NO RELIGION IS AN ISLAND

NO RELIGION IS AN ISLAND

The *Nostra Aetate* Dialogues

edited by
EDWARD BRISTOW

Fordham University Press
New York
1998

Library of Congress Cataloging-in-Publication Data

No religion is an island : the Nostra Aetate dialogues / edited by
Edward W. Bristow.
    p.   cm.
Based on a series of dialogues held at Fordham University.
Includes bibliographical references.
    ISBN 0–8232–1824–4 (alk. paper). — ISBN 0–8232–1825–2 (pbk. :
alk. paper)
    1. Judaism—Relations—Catholic Church—Congresses.   2. Catholic
Church—Relations—Judaism—Congresses.   3. Vatican Council (wnd :
1962–1965) Declaratio de ecclesiae habitudine ad religiones non
-Christianas—Congresses.   I. Bristow, Edward W.
BM535.N59   1998
261.2'6—dc21   98–38054
                                                                                              CIP

Printed in the United States of America

CONTENTS

Acknowledgements   vii

Preface   ix
    Joseph A. O'Hare, S.J.

West Side Story   1
    Burton L. Visotzky

A Catholic Perspective on *Nostra Aetate*   12
    Donald J. Moore, S.J.

The Jewishness of Jesus (November 10, 1993)   24
    Peter Steinfels
    John P. Meier
    Shaye J. D. Cohen

The Death of Jesus (November 17, 1994)   56
    Burton L. Visotzky
    Raymond E. Brown
    Michael J. Cook

Catholic-Jewish Dialogue and the New Millenium
    (November 20, 1995)   101
    Margaret Steinfels
    Ismar Schorsch
    His Eminence John Cardinal O'Connor

Jerusalem: Heavenly City and Earthly Center in Jewish
    and Early Christian Thought (November 14, 1996)   124
    Byron Shafer
    Robert Wilken
    Michael Fishbane

Abraham Joshua Heschel: Prophet of Social Activism
(November 10, 1997)   153
  John Healey
  Eugene Borowitz
  Daniel Berrigan, S.J.
  Susannah Heschel

Notes on Contributors   181

ACKNOWLEDGMENTS

The *Nostra Aetate* Dialogues at Fordham University very rapidly developed a large, faithful, and informed following. That we have consistently played to full houses and generated lengthy public exchange suggests that this permanent record of the first five annual programs will be of interest to all who are concerned with interfaith dialogue.

I would like to thank Fr. Joseph A O'Hare, S.J., for encouraging the creation of the series, and Dr. Robert Carrubba, Fordham's Vice President for Academic Affaris, for encouraging the publication of the proceedings. We are especially grateful to Mr. Kenneth Hickman and, too, the Louis Finkelstein Institute for Religious and Social Studies of the Jewish Theological Seminary for providing financial support for the book. Funders of the programs have included the J. Aron Charitable Foundation, the Summit Foundation, the Rabbi Marc H. Tanenbaum Foundation, and Mr. Sidney Rosenblatt. Fordham's co-sponsor for the series, the Jewish Community Center on the Upper West Side, has been instrumental in the considerable popularity of our annual programs.

All of the original presentations and exchanges have been annotated where appropriate, and several papers have been substantially expanded for publication. The sad news of Fr. Raymond Brown's death reached just before publication. Fr. Brown's contribution first appeared in *America*, April 1, 1995. After speaking at Fordham in November 1994, Fr. Brown recorded his thoughts in a systematic manner and they subsequently appeared in the Jesuit weekly. Fr. Brown asked that this paper form his contribution to the volume. Our title, which so aptly reflects the spirit of the dialogues, is borrowed from a 1966 lecture by Rabbi Abraham Joshua Heschel at the Union Theological Seminary.

EDWARD BRISTOW

PREFACE

Nearly ten years ago, when a committee of Fordham men and women began to plan the celebration of the University's Sesqui-centennial Anniversary in the school year 1990–1991, we all agreed that our celebration should not be simply an exercise in nostalgia. Instead, we were convinced that a year that celebrated 150 years of the University's existence should be the occasion for a renewal of our distinctive traditions. In other words, we believed that in a recovery of the best of our past, we would discover the key to a creative future. We hoped to capture this double perspective in the theme we selected for our Sesquicentennial Year: Fordham, After 150 Years, Keeping Faith with the Future.

In a year of memorable events, including a number of stimulating academic conferences, perhaps no single event captured the special focus of our Sesquicentennial celebration as profoundly as the two-day conference on the Catholic–Jewish dialogue held at both our Rose Hill and Lincoln Center campuses in September 1990. The occasion was the twenty-fifth anniversary of the seminal document of the Second Vatican Council on non-Christian religions, *Nostra Aetate*, a document that, participants agreed, had transformed the Jewish–Catholic dialogue. Elie Wiesel, the holocaust survivor, writer, and Nobel Peace Prize winner, delivered the keynote address for the conference and received an honorary degree from the University. Catholic and Jewish scholars, in a series of panel discussions, addressed the issues that continued to divide Catholics and Jews, even after 25 years of dialogue. Jewish leaders spoke with candor of their disappointment with *Nostra Aetate* and other Church documents that, while well intentioned, failed to fully respond to Jewish concerns about Christian prosyletism. Catholic scholars challenged the territorial claims of the State of Israel. At times, the conversations were tense and emotionally charged. Participants agreed, however, that honest disagreements had to be articulated and confronted if progress in the dialogue were to continue.

In his keynote address, Elie Wiesel had anticipated such disagreement and recognized its necessity. "Rapprochement means diversity, not uniformity. That is why rapprochement must never be attained at the expense of memory. Memory is the best and purest of links. Only if we remember shall we come closer to one another. Remember—and we will be dazzled to discover that for reasons known perhaps by God alone, our two communities have been locked in a cosmic drama that has affected history. Remember—and we shall learn to respect one another for what we are meant to be: a mirror to each other." Remembrance as a source of renewal was the underlying theme of our year-long Sesquicentennial celebration, and the Nostra Aetate conference was its most profound embodiment, since it tapped the deep religious roots that define Fordham University's distinctive identity and mission.

That same combination of religious passion and intellectual honesty has also characterized the series of Nostra Aetate Dialogues that have taken place at Fordham's Lincoln Center campus in the years following our Sesquicentennial celebration. In the pages that follow, you will find the record of those conversations, which have addressed, often in the most personal of terms, the issues that continue to divide Catholics and Jews as well as the hopes that unite them.

Three months ago, on March 16, 1998, the Pontifical Commission for Religious Relations with the Jews published at the Vatican a reflection on Catholic attitudes toward the Holocaust. Like previous Church documents, certainly including *Nostra Aetate* itself, the "reflection on the Shoah" disappointed many Jewish leaders. In Britain, the chief rabbi, Dr. Jonathan Sacks, said that the document spoke the language of "regret rather than apology." Writing in *America* magazine, the Rev. Avery Dulles, S.J., noted that the statement, like previous Vatican documents on the Holocaust, was both contrite and defensive in tone. The document's distinctions between the Church itself, which remains pure of any wrong-doing, and the members of the Church, who are always vulnerable to error and sin, was not completely persuasive to even Catholic commentators. Similarly, the distinction between anti-Judaism, which could be traced to misinterpretations of Catholic doctrine and practice, and anti-Semitism, which was born of the racist ideology of the Nazi movement, did not seem to consider seriously enough the extent to which religious anti-Judaism may have made racist anti-Semitism more acceptable.

But the very title of the Pontifical Commission's statement, "We Remember: A Reflection on the Shoah," echoed Elie Wiesel's call to remembrance at our Sesquicentennial conference eight years ago. "The common future of Jews and Christians," the Commission wrote, "demands that we remember, for 'there is no future without memory.' History itself is 'memoria futuri.'" We all reconstruct the past, whether personal or collective, from different angles of vision. The challenge of dialogue is often to work through different sets of memories to find ground for common hopes rather than continuing conflict. It is to this purpose that the Nostra Aetate Dialogues at Fordham University have been dedicated, and I offer my congratulations and gratitude to Dr. Edward Bristow and his colleagues for institutionalizing a conversation that demonstrates in so dramatic a fashion the convergence of religious faith and intellectual inquiry that is at the very center of the life of a Catholic university.

June 10, 1998

JOSEPH A. O'HARE, S.J.
President,
Fordham University

West Side Story

Burton L. Visotzky

As the second Christian millenium lumbers along like a Golem toward its end—the name of God emblazoned on its forehead, as it were, vivifying if not directing it—we pause to marvel at its very existence, even as we take stock of the enormous damage it has wrought. This last century has been the bloodiest of Christian history yet. The depredations wreaked on the Jews in the name of holy retribution have equaled those of all previous centuries combined. This was no mean feat, a source of perverse pride for the Aryan hordes. Their campaign to rid Europe of Jews had to match the violence of all crusades, expulsions, and pogroms past. They succeeded; in the wake of World War II there were one-third fewer Jews in the world. And so, even the advent of the State of Israel could not shake Jews from their conviction that militant Christian triumphalism made the followers of that rabbi from Nazareth dangerous enemies who would hound Judaism to its doom.

How surprising, then, that two decades after the war—only twenty years out of two thousand, a mere one percent of the Christian calendar—the Second Vatican Council would, in 1965, utterly redefine the relationship of the Church and the Jews. *Nostra Aetate*, the document on the relationship of the Church to non-Christian religions, was the noble vehicle of the Church's redefinition. Of course, after the Golem had run amok, perhaps it is not surprising at all that this change took place. For if the Church were to continue to claim a share in the name of God, the body of that Church could no longer be a Golem unfettered and instead had to learn to act the role of sister to the Judaism that also claimed God's holy name. And so, despite the two thousand years of bitter separation, Church and Synagogue found themselves like young sisters, warily, clumsily learning to embrace in an awkward dance called dialogue.

Dialogue was truly awkward, wary, and clumsy. The Church

did not always find the Jews willing partners in the dance, sometimes searching helplessly for Jews to talk with. The Jews, who
had once been crushed by the arms of the Golem, were under-
standably reluctant to enter any embrace with the Church. Of
course, there remain such Jews who disdain any contact with
goyim. Yet slowly, in the last three decades, there have been Jews
who have risen to the occasion and entered the careful choreography of mutual forgiveness. This is a difficult achievement, in and
of itself miraculous. For at the heart of Christian theology pre-
Nostra Aetate was the assumption that the Jews, as a people, bore
guilt. And among the Jews, there was not only incredulity at what
seemed to be a preposterous position, but equal laying of blame
on Christianity for the persecutions of the Jews throughout the
Christian centuries.

Nowhere was the scale of this mutual burden more apparent
than in Europe. Yet I personally have witnessed, on no less sacred
ground then at the death camp of Treblinka where 800,000 Jews
were gassed to death, a German Christian theologian beg both
God and the Jews who held his hands there: "Forgive us for our
sins." This watershed in Christian theology, so concretized in
Nostra Aetate, allows Jews and Christians to grope toward one
another, seeking forgiveness. Jews must be careful in this en-
deavor, for it is a temptation to withhold the very forgiveness that
Christianity now seeks. Further, Jews bristle at the suggestion that
they themselves need be forgiven anything by Christians. How
hard must it be for Christians, under these conditions, to continue
to reach out and invite dialogue.

In the United States, where the blood of Jews does not fertilize
the soil and where the ash of myriads of cremated Jews does not
reside in every Christian lung, in America the dialogue is much
less stilted. The freedom of religion celebrated by this Christian
country pretends to equality for all. Whatever the failings of that
freedom may be, the ethos nevertheless remains one of tolerance
and mutual respect. Without the freighted history of Europe, nor
the formal marriage of Church and State, dialogue between Jews
and Christians in America began well before *Nostra Aetate.* Indeed, it was sometimes easier for Christians to dialogue with Jews
than it was for various church denominations or for Protestants
and Catholics to dialogue with one another. In fact, for sixty years

now one of the premiere locations for ecumenical dialogue has
been at my home institution, the Jewish Theological Seminary.
There, Catholics, Protestants, Jews, and members of other faiths
learned to talk together about the great issues of the day.

But even with double the years of dialogue since *Nostra Aetate*,
even in America there are still detractors to dialogue. There are
Jews who view the Nazi horrors as unforgivable as well as unfor-
gettable. And there are Jews who, with or without recent Jewish
history, do not believe that it is the lot of Judaism to be anything
other than a nation set apart. But the vast majority of American
Jews, having forged their identities between the anvil and ham-
mer of Holocaust and Israeli military might, are ready to engage
their gentile neighbors. This dialogue serves as much to help
American Judaism define its own uniqueness here on this conti-
nent as it does to explain ourselves to our Christian counterparts.

Nowhere are Jews more comfortably massed than in New York
City. There are more Jews in the megapolis than in the State of
Israel. Further, the cultural output of New York Jewry is on a par
or surpasses even the greatest centers of Jewish life throughout
history. For many in this country, particularly those who live away
from either coast and dwell in the great, flat Christian heartland,
New York is synonymous with Judaism. Given this security of
numbers and cultural identity, interfaith dialogue in New York
achieves a complex choreography. Even when there is a clash or
disagreement, it is as elegant as a Jerome Robbins pas-de-deux.
To carry the metaphor one step further, let us add the music of
Leonard Bernstein, so that Jewish–Christian dialogue this last
half-decade in New York City is the "somewhere, some time,
some place" of *West Side Story*.

The core of *West Side Story*, both the movie and the dialogue,
is the West Sixties of Manhattan. There, not only did the Sharks
and Jets engage before the camera's eye, but Jews and Catholics
interacted at Fordham University's Lincoln Center Campus. The
five years of annual *Nostra Aetate* Dialogues that have taken place
there fly in the face of the lurking Golem. Rather than see the
monster looming before them, the Jews and Catholics who gather
at Fordham ever year focus on the emblazoned name of God and
its meaning for us, all God's creatures. In these dialogues there
has been a palpable sense that while the work of our human hands

may have wreaked havoc, there is a divine spark in the work of God's hands, and we who are created in God's image must nurture that spark. Thus the interchanges have been spirited, intellectual, and religious dialogues: "disagreements in the name of heaven." As the second century tractate *Pirque Avot* points out, such disagreements will sustain us and so, live on.

In the 1992–93 academic year I received a call from a friend of mine, a member of my synagogue whose daughter went to the Abraham Joshua Heschel School along with my daughter. This friend is a Professor of Comparative Literature at Fordham University. Anne Golomb Hoffman wanted me to join her and the Lincoln Center Campus dean for lunch to talk over a proposal regarding inter-faith dialogue. I assented and met Professor Ed Bristow, who as it turns out, is also Jewish. We sat over a meal near Lincoln Center, discussing how to best utilize a seed grant given to the Jesuit University by one of its Jewish alumni. It struck me as ironic that three Jews should be mulling how to spend a fourth Jew's money to promote Jewish-Catholic dialogue on behalf of a Catholic institution. I need not have worried, for once I agreed to participate, Dean Bristow gathered a planning committee of equal numbers of Jews and Catholics. Fordham University was an eager and active proponent of this dialogue. Indeed, since experience had taught me that sometimes it was the Jews who were reluctant to participate in such fora, I suggested that we invite the Jewish Community Center of the Upper West Side to be a co-sponsor. The Center accepted, and remains a proud partner in promoting the *Nostra Aetate* Dialogues.

We determined that November, before Thanksgiving, would be a good time of year to bring together the communities of the West Side to hear these interchanges. We further opted for a mixture of academic and popular tone in the dialogues, feeling that this was a community that would enjoy a high level of discourse. Further, we decided that both historical perspective as well as up-to-date issues were to be the agenda for these talks. Finally, while we desired interchange between two principal speakers, we also fixed a segment of each exchange for audience interaction. *Post facto*, when it was clear that these dialogues had created a treasure with a value far beyond the immediate needs of the Upper West

Side community, Dean Bristow determined to publish the proceedings for distribution to the widest possible audience.

For our first year we invited two eminent historians of the first
century to engage one another on "The Jewishness of Jesus."
Professor Shaye J. D. Cohen, Ungerleider Professor Judaic Studies at Brown University, is a renowned scholar of Josephus and
late antique Judaism. Cohen had for many years been professor at
the Jewish Theological Seminary and happily agreed to return to
his native New York to engage in conversation. The Catholic
representative was Fr. John Meier, a Professor of New Testament
at Catholic University in Washington, D.C. Professor Meier had
just published the first volume of his monumental *A Marginal Jew:
Rethinking the Historical Jesus* and so was ripe for the topic. But I
confess that I had a hidden reason for wishing Fr. Meier to engage
my fast-talking colleague, Rabbi Shaye Cohen.

Some years earlier Fr. Meier and I had met while consulting for
television. The network was planning a mini-series on the apostle
Paul and needed "scholarly consultants" to offer our *hekhsher*
(that's Jewish for imprimatur). We were taken to a fancy Italian
mid-town restaurant to soften us up before the viewing. Fr. Meier
had arrived in his clerical collar, which earned the silent disdain
of the network executive who was handling us. He turned with
a sneer to Fr. Meier and asked condescendingly if the good father
would, perhaps, wish to order the wine for the meal. John Meier
did not take umbrage. Rather, he turned to the Italian wine steward and engaged him in a rapid-fire dialogue in Italian, following
which the steward went off beaming to fetch the wine. When
Meier and I were heading home I expressed my appreciation of
both his Italian fluency and his knowledge of fine wines. Meier
was unflappable, "How could that fool from the network think I
would not know wine? I studied in Rome!"

Fr. Meier and Rabbi Cohen proved a delightful match for one
another. Moderated by Peter Steinfels, the urbane religion correspondent of *The New York Times*, the two scholars showed extraordinary good humor and wit as each gave hard-core, cutting-
edge scholarly presentations on the state of modern studies on
Jesus' Jewishness. There was a vigorous question-and-answer period in the overflowing auditorium. Respect for one another,
careful scholarship, and love of the subject matter became the

hallmark for the series as it was set on its way. I believe every member of the audience appreciated the significance of the moment. If that were not already apparent, the fact that Fordham, a Jesuit University, served a kosher reception afterward made the goodwill utterly palatable.

In the second year of dialogue, we remained in first-century history and scholarship. The success of the first year gave us a formula from which we were, as yet, reluctant to depart. We had the good fortune to hear from my own teacher, Fr. Raymond Brown. Professor Brown is the premiere New Testament scholar in America and had taught at the Protestant Union Theological Seminary for many years. We were able to coax him out of retirement in California to lecture in New York. His dialogue partner was Rabbi Michael Cook, Bronstein Professor of Judeo-Christian Studies at Hebrew Union College, the Reform Jewish Seminary in Cincinnati. Fr. Brown had recently published his magisterial *The Death of the Messiah*, and so was willing to engage on the potentially prickly topic "The Death of Jesus."

As will be clear to all who read the treatment of the subject in this volume, the dialogue that night pulled no punches. Brown hewed to what he had determined as historic fact, even as he bemoaned the ways in which those facts had been employed to abuse the Jews for centuries. Rabbi Cook, for his part, concurred in large part with Brown's historic findings. But he was quick to remind the audience of the dire consequences those readings of the New Testament have had for the Jews throughout history. The audience interaction that followed was predictably careful and uncomfortable. Yet, again, the goodwill of the combined Jews and Christians in the audience made it clear that even on so difficult an issue as the death of Jesus, progress could be made in Catholic–Jewish dialogue. The *Nostra Aetate* Dialogues had now earned their name.

The series had now been firmly established. For two years running, there were huge audiences on scholarly historic topics. And, for two years running, the goodwill of the series had allowed scholars to tackle difficult issues in a spirit of open interchange and learning. All who participated were affected by these dialogues. In that spirit we moved to the modern era for our third dialogue, bringing together the head of the Catholic community of New

York with one of the great leaders of the more disparate Jewish community. His Eminence John Cardinal O'Connor, Archbishop of New York, was to engage Rabbi Ismar Schorsch, Chancellor of the Conservative Jewish Theological Seminary on the future of interreligious dialogue.

Each of these leaders has an influence far beyond New York City, and we had hoped that their engagement would set a tone for "Catholic-Jewish Dialogue and the New Millenium." I confess to have been disappointed with the result. Each leader spoke eloquently about engagement with the other religion. Each alluded to the past. Each recounted areas of progress and areas where the religions separately were placing their energies. Each respectfully suggested areas for future cooperation. Perhaps it is a great sign of progress since *Nostra Aetate* was first published in 1965 or perhaps it is a result of the two minorities, Jewish and Catholic, enjoying so much clout in New York—but there was no conflict between these two leaders of religions that had been one another's nemesis for so many centuries. There was practically no disagreement whatsoever. What might have been a respectful—even good-humored—argument seemed, instead, a love feast.

Only in the question-and-answer period did either of these giants depart from singing in harmony. At least, that is my recollection. Perhaps the reader of the transcripts published here will find my memory faulty. But as I recollect the Schorsch–O'Connor evening I hear a harmony that is either forced or bodes extremely well for the coming decades. I pray, of course, for the latter.

Year four of the dialogue celebrated the three thousandth anniversary of the founding of Jerusalem. Having decided to focus on Jerusalem, the planning committee was divided on how to have a dialogue. There was a strong sentiment that any dialogue on Jerusalem must consider the Islamic presence there. "Jerusalem: Heavenly City and Earthly Center" seemed to demand that the dialogue now include a Muslim participant. In the end, however, the Catholic–Jewish mission of the series prevailed. We reluctantly confined the topic to "Jewish and Early Christian Thought." To this day I wonder if we were derelict in our interreligious mission. But having limited the scope of the dialogue once again to Jews and Catholics, two extraordinary scholars were brought for conversation.

Dr. Robert Wilken, Kenan Professor of the History of Christianity at the University of Virginia, is the author of a book, *The Land Called Holy*, which studies the Christianization of Palestine in the first six centuries of this era. His counterpart was Dr. Michael Fishbane, Cummings Professor of Jewish Studies at the University of Chicago. As will be clear from the transcripts which follow, the erudition of these two great scholars is matched only by their good will in interacting. I personally have witnessed Professor Wilken lean back in his chair at a conference in Jerusalem and quote (in Hebrew) a rabbinic dictum to an Israeli scholar reading a paper on the Crusades. This urbane breadth of knowledge is readily matched by Fishbane's own far-reaching and influential studies. Listeners and now readers will be treated to a dialogue of intellectual history with Jerusalem as its focus. Rarely has the holy city generated as much dazzling insight, especially given its history as a battleground.

The fifth and most recent dialogue commemorated the twenty-fifth anniversary of the death of the revered theologian Rabbi Abraham Joshua Heschel. Heschel's work is widely read in both the Jewish and Christian communities. His impact in his lifetime was all the greater through his activism in the great social causes of the day. Rabbi Heschel was a deeply observant Jew who passionately engaged in the civil rights marches and anti-war protests of the 1960s up until his death in 1972. I had the privilege of meeting with him and hearing him speak many times at the Jewish Theological Seminary. To commemorate this great religious leader and thinker and to make clear that his example was to be emulated, the committee fixed the topic for the dialogue, "Abraham Joshua Heschel: Prophet of Social Activism."

For the first time, the structure of two speakers and a moderator was changed. In order to both pay homage to Heschel's memory and to look to the future, a new format was proposed. This format continued to have a Jew and a Catholic as the principal speakers, but now a Protestant moderator was invited to join with yet another Jew who would serve as a respondent to the formal lectures. The moderator was to have been Ms. Yolanda King, daughter of the late Dr. Martin Luther King. The respondent was Dr. Susannah Heschel, Eli Black Professor of Jewish Studies at Dartmouth College and daughter of the late Rabbi Heschel.

In the end, Ms. King was unable to attend at the last moment; an able pinch-hitter was found in Dr. John Healey, director of Fordham's Archbishop Hughes Institute. The two opening speakers were Fr. Daniel Berrigan, S.J., who had been a friend of Heschel's and a well-known activist himself. The Jewish speaker was Rabbi Eugene Borowitz, Falk Professor of Jewish Religious Thought at the Reform movement's Hebrew Union College. Rabbi Borowitz offered not only a rationale for Heschel's activism, but attempted as well to explain the parameters of that activism within the confines of Jewish law and thought. Borowitz, once a student of Heschel's, offered an apologetic for Heschel's refusal to engage in civil disobedience, one of the chief methods of protest of those times and a method heartily embraced by Berrigan.

For his part, Fr. Berrigan was low-key, reminiscing about his friendship with Heschel. Yet Berrigan was predictably provocative, both with his ferocious polemic against the Nixon government and his attendant criticism of Israel and American Jewry at the time. I recall that in the late sixties there was a great deal of suspicion in the Jewish community of Fr. Berrigan. Although overwhelming numbers of us sympathized with his anti-war activities (Heschel included), there were many who questioned the sincerity of his professed friendship with the Jews. No doubt this was prompted by his criticisms of Israel (which now seem mainstream). Yet these suspicions of Berrigan's friendship were exacerbated on the night of the dialogue when he proclaimed his assent to the proposition that friendship must extend to all humanity—even Hitler.

I leave it to the reader's pleasure to savor the delicacy of Professor Susannah Heschel's response to Fr. Berrigan. In her remarks about her father she not only offered a corrective to Rabbi Borowitz's theorizing about the limits of late Rabbi Heschel's activism, but admonished Berrigan regarding the necessity of sincerity in true friendship. The Hasidic tale she quoted in reproof of Fr. Berrigan made it eminently clear that Rabbi Heschel's mantle of Jewish leadership rests firmly on his daughter Susannah's shoulders. It is she who is the "rebbe" of Jewish social activism for the younger generation.

What, then, is the agenda for future dialogues? How can the younger generation join hands with its elders in continued dialogue? There are still many historic topics to be explored. So far, the *Nostra Aetate* dialogues have not taken up the Apostle Paul, an essential legacy of the Church with far-reaching implications for both Christian theology and the history of interaction with the Jews.[1] In the same vein, the legacy of the Church fathers merits careful consideration. The virulence of attacks from such figures as St. John Chrysostom must be placed within historic perspective. So, too, alas, the history of Church persecutions of the Jews throughout the Middle Ages and the Inquisition. Sadly, we must add to the weight of all this sorry history the role of the Roman Catholic Church in the Holocaust.

We must also address social issues which demand delicate consideration not only of the topic but of one another, Jew and Catholic. Here I refer to such hot topics as abortion, women's ordination, parochial versus public schooling, and the role of church versus state in the provision of a safety net for those in our American society without financial resources. Just beneath the surface of this discussion is the prickly topic of our vision of America in the future. Do we desire a secular society for the next saeculum or do we envision a country guided by Judeo-Christian values? If this latter question seems innocuous, imagine if we frame it: should America be a Christian country? The rephrasing is, I fear, often the real query behind those who link the more politically correct term "Judeo-Christian" with an insistence on imposing their values on others. Both the Jewish and Catholic minorities of this country should remember their wariness about the "tyranny of the majority" of half a century ago.

It is with a great deal of pride that I conclude this introduction to these five years of *Nostra Aetate* dialogues—pride at having been on the program committee, pride at being part of an incredibly vibrant Jewish community that is an equal partner in these essen-

---

[1] This became the theme for the dialogue of November 1998 (editor's note).

tial dialogues, and pride at being a professor at the Jewish Theological Seminary, one of the co-sponsors of this publication. My pride and thanks chiefly extend to our sister institution, Fordham University at Lincoln Center, to former Dean Bristow and to Fordham's President, Fr. Joseph A. O'Hare, S.J., for sponsoring these dialogues. Fordham continues to grow in greatness as both a religious and an academic institution through the *Nostra Aetate* Dialogues. In the words of the Psalmist, "May you go from strength to strength. . . ."

A Catholic Perspective on *Nostra Aetate*

Donald J. Moore, S.J.

In the thirty plus years that have elapsed since the close of Vatican II, we have witnessed a profound change in the Catholic Church's attitude toward other world religions. Vatican II encouraged the Church to take a more vigorous participation in the area of interreligious dialogue and even to move, if ever so slowly, toward that ideal cherished by Karl Rahner, the ideal of becoming truly a world church. Obviously, *Gaudium et Spes* (*Constitution on the Church in the Modern World*) played a major role in this transformation. Much credit, however, must also be given to *Nostra Aetate* (Declaration on the Relation of the Church to Non-Christian Religions), the briefest official document stemming from the Council. The ideals expressed in *Nostra Aetate* have helped to initiate a continual renewal of the Church's self-understanding as it seeks to clarify its relationships to other religions.

CONTRIBUTION OF *NOSTRA AETATE*

Nostra Aetate urges all Christians, while witnessing to their own faith and way of life, to "acknowledge, preserve and encourage the spiritual and moral truths" found in other world religions (*Nostra Aetate* No. 2). This challenge was taken up in a specific way by the 34th General Congregation of the Society of Jesus, especially in Decree No. 5, which calls on all members of the Society to respect the plurality of religions as "the human response to God's salvific work in peoples and cultures. Interreligious dialogue at its deepest level is always a dialogue of salvation, because it seeks to discover, clarify, and understand better the signs of the age-long dialogue which God maintains with humanity

[John Paul II]. An open and sincere interreligious dialogue is our cooperation with God's ongoing dialogue with humanity."[1]

If this holds true for all world religions, it is especially true of the Church's dialogue with Jews and Judaism. *Nostra Aetate*, primarily through its section devoted to Judaism, has been responsible for an extraordinary change in attitude between Jews and Christians. It provided possibilities for dialogue between Jews and Christians that had never before existed in the history of these two great religions. *Nostra Aetate* reminds us that Christians and Jews have a deep common "spiritual heritage"; there are unique spiritual ties "which link the people of the New Covenant to the stock of Abraham," for the Church continues to draw nourishment "from that good olive tree onto which the wild branches of the Gentiles have been grafted" (*Nostra Aetate* No. 4). These last thirty years have also witnessed what the late Jan Cardinal Willebrands had labeled "a real, almost miraculous conversion" in the attitudes of Jews and Catholics toward one another.[2] And Cardinal Edward Cassidy, current head of the Vatican Commission for Religious Relations with the Jews, claims that Catholic–Jewish relations are now "better than they had ever been during the two thousand years of Christianity."[3]

Unfortunately, for the greater part of these two thousand years Jews and Christians had nurtured critically opposing images of one another. From the Christian perspective, Jews belonged to a superseded religion, a religion whose purpose was to prepare the way for the Messiah and to give birth to Christianity, a religion blind to the fulfillment of its own prophecies, a religion whose covenant with God had come to an end. From the Jewish perspective, Christianity represented a deviant outgrowth and dilution of the best insights of Judaism, a religion whose adherents were responsible for the crusades, the pogroms, the ghettos, and who were all too silent during the years of Hitler's "Final Solution."

---

[1] *Documents of the Thirty-Fourth Congregation of the Society of Jesus* (St Louis: The Institute of Jesuit Sources, 1995), pp. 70–71.

[2] Cited in Thomas Stransky, "The Catholic-Jewish Dialogue: Twenty Years after *Nostra Aetate*," in *America*, February 8, 1986, p. 93.

[3] Edward Cardinal Cassidy, "The Next Issues in Jewish-Christian Relations," *Origins* 26 (April 3, 1997), p. 667.

FROM MISTRUST TO COLLABORATION

Such negative concepts, rooted so often in mistrust and contempt, are now giving way to new understandings that spring from genuine dialogue, from a deepening respect for each other's faith commitment, from the growing recognition that both Jews and Christians are called to live in fidelity to their covenant with God. Jews and Christians, often for the first time, are truly seeking to learn from one another and to collaborate with one another in solving the social and political problems that have brought such profound misery to so many people in the closing decades of this century.

The most prominent contributor to these new understandings, at least from the Catholic side, has been Pope John Paul II. On so many occasions and in so many ways the Pontiff has energetically pushed forward the agenda of Vatican II and especially of *Nostra Aetate*. He has urged Catholics to acquire a deeper appreciation of how Jews define themselves in the light of their own religious experience; at the same time he has pointed to the need of the Church to reinterpret its relationship to Jews as the people of God. In one of his first meetings with Jewish leaders the Pope stressed that the spiritual bond linking Jews and Christians implied that "our two religious communities are connected and closely related at the very level of their respective religious identities" and so the path along which we should proceed "is one of fraternal dialogue and fruitful collaboration."[4] At another such meeting he asserted that "whoever meets Jesus Christ meets Judaism" and that the meeting between Catholics and Jews is not one between present and past, as though the former had superseded the latter; rather, it "is the meeting of the people of God of the Old Covenant, never revoked by God, and that of the New Covenant."[5]

One of the strongest and clearest remarks of John Paul II was made during his historic visit to the Synagogue of Rome in 1986. "The Jewish religion is not 'extrinsic' to us, but in a certain way is 'intrinsic' to our own religion. With Judaism therefore we have

---

[4] Eugene Fisher and Leon Klenicki, eds., *Pope John Paul II on Jews and Judaism: 1979–1986* (Washington, D.C.: U.S. Catholic Conference), p. 24.

[5] Ibid., pp. 33, 35.

a relationship which we do not have with any other religion. You are our dearly beloved brothers [and sisters] and, in a certain way, it could be said that you are our elder brothers [and sisters]."[6] On the tenth anniversary of this historic visit, John Paul reminded Rome's chief rabbi, Elio Toaff, of the "atmosphere of sincere friendship that has been established between us, the sentiments of fraternal caring for one another that motivate us. . . . [O]ur brotherhood," he went on to say, "is all the more real insofar as it is rooted in a common spiritual heritage that is extraordinarily rich and profound. The new spirit of friendship and mutual concern which marks Catholic–Jewish relations can be the most important sign that Jews and Catholics have to offer a restless world. . . ."[7] One final example: in an address to the Jewish community in Poland on the occasion of the fiftieth anniversary of the Warsaw Ghetto uprising, the Pope reminded his listeners: "As Christians and Jews, following the example of the faith of Abraham, we are called to be a blessing for the world (cf. Genesis 12:2ff). This is a common task awaiting us. It is therefore necessary for us, Christians and Jews, to be first a blessing to one another."[8] Clearly, John Paul II has exerted dynamic leadership and taken great pains to help efface the stereotypical views of Judaism espoused by so many Christians.

Mention should also be made of some of the outstanding efforts by Jewish intellectuals, especially in this century, to spell out this unique relationship between Judaism and Christianity, a relationship often perceived to be rooted primarily in Jesus. Rabbi Leo Baeck saw Jesus as a "God-sent personality," a "Jew among Jews," for whom Judaism has nothing but "love and respect." From no other people could Jesus have emerged, from no other people could he have found the apostles who believed in him, among no other people could he have been so active.[9] Franz Rosenzweig agreed with the Christian assertion that no one can come to God except through Christ, but Jews have no need to

---

[6] Ibid., p. 82

[7] John Paul II, "Remarks to Rome's Chief Rabbi," *Origins* 26 (May 23, 1996), p. 9.

[8] John Paul II, as cited in Cassidy, p. 670.

[9] Fritz Rothschild, ed., *Jewish Perspectives on Christianity* (New York: Crossroads, 1990), p. 44.

come to God, for through the Covenant they are already *with* God.[10] Abraham Heschel called upon Jews to ponder the role that the Church has played, and continues to play, in God's plan for the redemption of all nations; Jews should acknowledge "with a grateful heart" that it was the Church that made the Hebrew Bible available to all humankind, thus bringing to the whole world the knowledge of the God of Abraham, Isaac, and Jacob.[11] And of course Martin Buber refers to Jesus as "my great brother" with whom I have had a "fraternally open relationship" that has grown "ever stronger and clearer" in the passing years.[12] For Buber Jesus is a Jew to the core, so that Jews have a knowledge of Jesus inaccessible to the non-Jew, a knowledge of Jesus "from within," from the impulses and stirrings of his Jewishness[13] Buber would have strongly endorsed the remark of John Paul II: "Whoever meets Jesus Christ meets Judaism." Jesus for Buber represented in many ways the ideal of Judaism: he was a loyal son of Israel, the embodiment of the authentic faith of the prophets. On the other hand, John Paul has in his own way implicitly confirmed the truth of Buber's vision expressed fifteen years prior to *Nostra Aetate*, namely, that Judaism and Christianity "have something as yet unsaid to say to each other and a help to give one another . . . hardly to be conceived at the present time."[14]

A COMMON SPIRITUAL HERITAGE

One of the primary tasks of the Catholic–Jewish dialogue, emphasized both by *Nostra Aetate* and by Pope John Paul II, is to deepen our understanding of the common spiritual heritage that we share. Certainly the area of biblical studies continues to provide so much potential for exploring our common spiritual heritage. Yet there are many other sources which deserve

---

[10] Ibid., pp. 171–72.

[11] Cf. Donald Moore, *The Human and the Holy: The Spirituality of Abraham Joshua Heschel* (New York: Fordham University Press, 1989), pp. 166ff.

[12] Martin Buber, *Two Types of Faith* (New York: Harper Torchbooks, 1961), p. 12.

[13] Martin Buber, *Between Man and Man* (New York: Macmillan, 1965), p. 5.

[14] Buber, *Two Types of Faith*, p. 174.

investigation and which provide promise for deepening this common understanding of Jews and Christians.

One small example of this is a compelling summary of Hasidic insights from the pen of Martin Buber called "The Way of Man." There are two themes pervading these and other pages of Buber's Hasidic writings which have a close affinity to Christian and, more particularly, to Ignatian spirituality: the Hasidic emphases on the uniqueness of each person and on the hallowing of all things.[15]

UNIQUENESS OF EACH PERSON

In chapter two of "The Way of Man" Buber skillfully employs the use of Hasidic tales and aphorisms to stress a basic Hasidic teaching expressed by Rabbi Pinhas of Koretz: "In everyone there is something precious which is in no one else."[16] There is no single way of developing this preciousness. The Seer of Lublin remarked: "It is impossible to tell men what way they should take. For one way to serve God is through learning, another through prayer, another through fasting, and still another through eating. Everyone should carefully observe what way his heart draws him to, and then choose this way with all his strength."[17] We can learn from the great spiritual leaders within our traditions, we should study their achievements, but we should not try simply to imitate them lest we miss what we, and we alone, are called upon to do. There is something so refreshing and so healthily counter-cultural in Buber's exposition of Hasidic tales and aphorisms in "The Way of Man." For example, there is the wisdom of the aged Rabbi Bunham: "I should not like to change places with our father Abraham! What good would it do God if Abraham became like blind Bunham, and blind Bunham like Abra-

---

[15] A fuller development of these ideas can be found in Donald Moore, "An Ignatian Perspective on Contemporary Jewish Spirituality," *Thought*, LXVII (Dec. 1992), pp. 420–29.

[16] Martin Buber, *Tales of the Hasidim: Early Masters* (New York: Schocken, 1961), p. 127.

[17] Buber, "The Way of Man" in *Hasidism and Modern Man* (New York: Harper Torchbooks, 1966), p. 138.

ham? Rather than have this happen, I think I shall try to become a little more myself." In the same vein Rabbi Susya remarks: "In the world to come I shall not be asked: 'Why were you not Moses?' I shall be asked: 'Why were you not Susya?'"[18]

Each one of us is unique and unprecedented. No matter how trivial our achievements might seem in comparison to others, "they have their real value in that we bring them about in our own way and by our own efforts."[19] This is the insight expressed by Menahem Mendel of Kotzk (the Kotzker): "Everything in the world can be imitated except truth. For truth that is imitated is no longer truth."[20] Buber expresses this Hasidic teaching: "Every person born into this world represents something new, something that never existed before, something original and unique. . . . Every man's foremost task is the actualization of his unique, unprecedented and never-recurring potentialities, and not the repetition that another, and be it even the greatest, has already achieved."[21] Each one of us should be able to say: there has never been anyone like me in the world, for if there had been someone like me, there would be no reason for me to be. Abraham Heschel puts it more simply: "With every child born a new expectation enters the world."[22]

There is then in everyone something precious that is found in no other. This preciousness is one's uniqueness. To live one's uniqueness is to respond to that personal vocation given to each of us by God in calling us into being. This closely corresponds to that which is at the heart of the Spiritual Exercises of St. Ignatius Loyola, namely, the "Election," which can be understood either as the discernment of the state of life to which one is called by God (what is it that God expects of me?) or as the reformation

---

[18] Ibid., p. 140. One might compare the intent of these remarks with the insight of David Stanley that in the light of the Spiritual Exercises of St. Ignatius Loyola it is clear that the Christian vocation is "to be thoroughly human, to be most truly myself." (In *A Modern Scriptural Approach to the Spiritual Exercises* [Chicago: Loyola University Press, 1967], p. 282).

[19] Buber, ibid., p. 139.

[20] Buber, *Tales of the Hasidim: Later Masters* (New York: Schocken, 1961), p. 284.

[21] Buber, *Hasidism and Modern Man*, pp. 139–40.

[22] Abraham Heschel, *Who Is Man?* (Stanford: Stanford University Press, 1965), p. 108.

within an already chosen state of life so that one gives oneself more completely to the demands of God on one's life. St. Ignatius refers to the Exercises as "every way of preparing and disposing the soul to rid itself of all inordinate attachments and, after their removal, of seeking and finding the will of God in the disposition of my life for the salvation of my soul" (Puhl, *Spiritual Exercises*, p. 1). Herbert Alphonso writes that the most profound and authentic meaning of Ignatius' "Election" is the discernment of one's "truest and deepest 'self,'" and this truest and deepest self is one's "God-given *uniqueness*" or what he also calls one's "Personal Vocation." In other words, at its deepest level, to find God's will in the disposition of my life is to find "my unrepeatable *uniqueness*,"[23] the very ideal expressed by the Hasidic masters. And the method of Ignatius' discernment finds its parallel in the wisdom of the Hasidim as summarized by Buber: we realize our uniqueness only through the knowledge of our own being, the knowledge of our essential qualities and inclinations. The precious something within us is revealed to us if we truly perceive our strongest feeling, our central wish, that in us which stirs our inmost being.[24]

FINDING GOD IN ALL THINGS

We develop our preciousness/uniqueness not ultimately for our own sake, but for the world's sake. An Hasidic spirituality begins with self but it does not end with self. There are two types of persons, says Rabbi Bunham, the proud who, even in the most sublime form, think only of themselves, and the humble who in all things think only of the world. There is the story of Rabbi Hayyim, who is so worried that he has not yet atoned that as a result his hair turns white. The advice of Rabbi Eliezer to him: stop wasting your energy on self-reproach and apply it instead to that active relationship with the world which is destined for you.[25] The conversion and repentance which are demanded of each of

---

[23] Herbert Alphonso, *The Personal Vocation* (Rome: Centrum Ignatianum Spiritualitatis, 1990), pp. 14, 18.

[24] Buber, *Hasidism and Modern Man*, p. 142.

[25] Ibid., pp. 163, 166.

us mean breaking away from the web of selfishness in which we are entangled and finding our way to God, that is, to the accomplishment of God's goals in our world. The atoner in this Hasidic tale is too concerned with his own personal salvation, a concern which is perhaps the most sublime form of that pride or self-centeredness mentioned by Rabbi Bunham.

Buber emphasizes the same point with this Hasidic aphorism: "God says to everyone as he said to Moses: 'Put off thy shoes from off thy feet'—put off the habitual which encloses your foot and you will recognize that the place on which you happen to be standing at this moment is holy ground."[26] The fulfillment of our existence, the fulfillment of our unique role in the world, is to be found in only one place, the place where we are standing here and now. Thus, the story of Rabbi Eizik, son of Rabbi Yekel of Cracow: He had a recurring dream to go to Prague, where he would find a treasure under the bridge leading to the king's palace. Rabbi Eizik makes the long trek to Prague, walks around and around the bridge, and finally the captain of the guard asks him what he is looking for. Eizik tells him of his dream and the captain laughs and tells of a dream of his own in which he was to go to Cracow and dig for a treasure under the stove in the room of a Jew, Eizik, son of Yekel. "I can just imagine what it would be like, how I would have to try every house over there, where one half of the Jews are named Eizik and the other Yekel!" The captain laughed again; Eizik bowed, traveled home, and there was the treasure under the stove in his room.

This is an old story, popular in a number of traditions, but the Hasidic treatment is quite clear: there is something that can be found only in one place, that great treasure known as the fulfillment of existence; it is found in the place where one stands here and now. We tend to search for this fulfillment in various provinces of the world or of the mind, but it can be found only here where we stand, where we have been set. As Buber expresses it: "The environment which I feel to be the natural one, the situation which has been assigned to me as my fate, the things that claim me day after day—these contain my essential task and such fulfillment of existence as is open to me." If we had power over

---

[26] Martin Buber, *Ten Rungs* (New York: Schocken, 1947), p. 15.

the ends of the earth, it would not give us that fulfillment of existence available by a quiet, devoted relationship to life at hand. If we perform with holy intent the tasks of our daily lives, we will realize indeed that "our treasure is hidden beneath the hearth of our own home."[27] If we can develop authentic relationships with, and be present to, the persons and things that belong to our world, then each encounter opens to a deeper, more spiritual significance. All things call out to us to liberate the divine spark found within them, and we do this by our relationships with them. One hallows all that one does by living with all things in a spirit of reverence. Each deed becomes redemptive according to the degree of presence with which one acts. Thus, a disciple of Moshe of Kobryn was asked: "What was most important to your teacher?" The response: "Whatever he happened to be doing at the moment."[28] And Rabbi Pinhas of Koretz told his disciples that there are no actions which in themselves are useless, but one can make them useless by "doing them uselessly."[29]

What is key here is our relationship to the things and persons of our life. Hasidism insists that if faith means *anything*, it must shape our attitude toward *everything*: this paper, this place, this person, this moment. One hallows the things of this world by a relationship of presence that is open to the transcendent. It is not primarily our knowledge or power or technology that forms the marrow of our human existence, but our relationships. "In the beginning is the relation," writes Buber in *I and Thou* (69). In other words, it is the personal that really counts. Hasidism for Buber emphasizes the living power of meeting and the living power of presence. A person is fully human, fully alive, when fully present. Buber believed that all Hasidic teaching could be summed up in one sentence: "God can be beheld in each thing and reached through each pure deed." And he continues: "no thing can exist without a divine spark, and each person can uncover and redeem this spark at each time and through each pure action, even the most ordinary, if only he performs it in purity, wholly directed to God and concentrated in Him. Therefore, it

---

[27] Buber, *Hasidism and Modern Man*, pp. 170–73.
[28] Buber, *Tales: Later Masters*, p. 173.
[29] Ibid., p. 122.

will not do to serve God only in isolated hours and with set words and gestures. One must serve God with one's whole life, with the whole of the everyday, with the whole of reality."[30]

Hasidism challenges us to accept the task of hallowing all things, of entering into genuine relation with all things, to do all that one does with the whole of one's being. It insists that we cannot approach God by reaching beyond the human; we can approach God only through becoming human; to become human is what we have been created for. "This, so it seems to me," writes Buber, "is the eternal core of Hasidic life and of Hasidic teaching."[31]

These Hasidic insights closely parallel the apex of Ignatian spirituality, and in a sense the apex of all Christian spirituality: finding God in all things. Father Jerome Nadal writes of Ignatius that "in all things, in every action or conversation, he was aware of God's presence. In a word he was *simul in actione contemplivus* —contemplative even while engaged in action, a habit that he was accustomed to explain while remarking: 'God must be found in all things.'"[32] For one formed in the Spiritual Exercises long periods of formal prayer ought not be necessary; rather, one should find God in all that one does. Prayer or contemplation leads one to engage oneself in God's plan for the redemption of the world, and this engagement, carried out with "*devotio*—commitment—commitment of the whole person," leads one back again to God.[33] And Father Peter-Hans Kolvenbach points out that "at the end of the Spiritual Exercises it is apparent that there is no other possibility of seeking and finding God, and of living His life, than to insert oneself fully, each in the place which, in the Election, he has found to be his own, in the ongoing history of the world . . . to seek and find God in all things, becoming one with them."[34]

There are many other fruitful comparisons to be made in the spiritual messages of the Hasidim and of St. Ignatius. These, how-

---

[30] Buber, *Hasidism and Modern Man*, pp. 49–50.

[31] Ibid., p. 43.

[32] Stanley, *Modern Scriptural Approach*, p. 149.

[33] Ibid., p. 154.

[34] Peter-Hans Kolvenbach, "Politics and Mysticism in Ignatius of Loyola" in *Ignatiana*, June 1991, p. 1.

ever, should be sufficient to indicate that many Jewish authors, by their interpretation and understanding of the wisdom of their own tradition, have much to offer us Christians as we strive to witness to the meaning of our humanness, our uniqueness, our own covenant of faith with God, as we strive to find God in all that we do. And it should be clear that we Christians do continue, as *Nostra Aetate* reminded us, to draw great nourishment from "that good olive tree," from the rich spiritual traditions of Israel, onto which we have been grafted.

The Jewishness of Jesus

November 10, 1993

Peter Steinfels: It really is remarkable that the title of tonight's program is the Jewishness of Jesus. This title seems to retain some degree of shock value, and it is indeed almost hard to imagine, but true, that not everyone recognizes that Jesus was a Jew. For non-Jews that fact is to be attributed to many things: to the personal or group egoism that recasts Jesus in one's own image, culture, and mind set; perhaps to the power of Jesus' person or message which leads to a firm identification with him; and finally, perhaps, to the toxins of anti-Semitism that have stained and twisted Christian history in its secular epilogues.

Elisabeth Schusler Fiorenza, in her study entitled *In Memory of Her* (New York: Crossroads, 1983), describes the difficulty that a friend of hers had in convincing an adult education class in a Catholic parish that Jesus was a Jew. The teacher, after some effort, had no sooner won a reluctant assent that Jesus was indeed a Jew than somebody spoke up: "But for sure the blessed mother is not." For most of two millennia Christianity has largely defined itself, and therefore Jesus, over against Judaism. Judaism in its own way often defined itself against Christianity.

Spurred by a combination of bold scholarship in our time and deep horror at the consequences of this self-serving antithesis, religious thinkers and authorities have insisted that we must abandon this habit and re-examine our views of Jesus. Jesus was a Jew. He was born a Jew, raised a Jew, understood himself in terms of the Jewish scriptures, spoke as a Jew to other Jews, preached his message in Jewish terms, proclaimed the message within Judaism and reportedly died with the label Jew—the charge indeed that he claimed to be no less than king of the Jews—affixed to the instrument of execution.

The recognition in our times of the Jewishness of Jesus has forced all of us, as well as historians, theologians, pastors, teachers, and religious authorities in both Jewish and Christian traditions, to look with fresh eyes on this Galilean teacher and healer, and at the movement that formed around his life and message. The impact of that recognition on our understanding of Jesus seems irreversible. Looking with fresh eyes means raising fresh questions as well as venturing fresh answers. Tonight, two outstanding scholars will give us an overview of both questions and answers.

John P. Meier: At least in academic circles, the assertion "Jesus was a Jew" has become a cliché. Once it was a controversial challenge and a spur to debate. Now it is so universally accepted that heads nod in drowsiness as well as in agreement. The problem is that many fail to grasp that the assertion "Jesus was a Jew" not only answers one question but also raises another.

If Jesus was a Jew, then *what kind* of Jew was he? The splendid work of distinguished scholars like Dr. Shaye Cohen and Jacob Neusner—and, on the Christian side, Morton Smith and E. P. Sanders—has made us reject the idea of any sort of monolithic, normative, or Orthodox Judaism in the early first century of the Common Era.[1] Judaism at the turn of the era was a rich religious tapestry of many threads and colors, a religion whose vitality was evidenced by the number of different tendencies and groups within it. So varied was the Judaism of the time that some scholars, like Dr. Neusner, have preferred to speak of Judaisms in the plural.[2]

Yet, for all its diversity, Judaism, while not having a neat monolithic character, did have, in my view, a mainstream. In this, I am close to the view espoused by Dr. Sanders in his recent book *Judaism: Practice and Belief*. While not easily definable, this mainstream is detectable in the fact that the vast majority of Jews were

---

[1] Among the many writings of these scholars see, e.g., Shaye J. D. Cohen, *From the Maccabees to the Mishnah* (Philadelphia: Westminster, 1987); Jacob Neusner, *Judaism in the Beginning of Christianity* (Philadelphia: Fortress, 1984); Morton Smith, *Jesus the Magician* (San Francisco: Harper & Row, 1978); E. P. Sanders, *Judaism: Practice and Belief, 63 BCE–66CE* (London: SCM; Philadelphia: Trinity, 1992).

[2] See the volume he edited along with William Scott Green and Ernest S. Frerichs, *Judaisms and Their Messiahs at the Turn of the Christian Era* (Cambridge: Cambridge University Press, 1987); also Jacob Neusner, "The Mishnah in Philosophical Context and out of Canonical Bounds," *Journal of Biblical Literature* 112 (1993), pp. 291–304.

committed to a sense of peoplehood and election, made concrete by observance of the Mosaic Law, especially as regards circumcision, the Sabbath, and the food laws, and by reverence for the temple in Jerusalem. This reverence for the temple was expressed in practice by contributions to its upkeep and by participation, insofar as possible, in the regular cycle of liturgical sacrifices, carried out by legitimate priests, with the high priest as the people's religious leader. Individuals may not have liked the particular high priest in office or the way he ran the temple, but reverence for the temple, the feasts of pilgrimage, the sacrifices, the priesthood, and the office of high priest ran deep among Jews both in the Diaspora and *a fortiori* in Judea and Galilee.

It is within this broad mainstream of Judaism that Dr. Cohen has placed Jesus the Jew, and to a great degree I affirm what he has said. But, granted this broad mainstream, which embraced all sorts of differences, the question becomes all the more pressing: What kind of Jew was Jesus? Where on the variegated map of first-century Palestinian Judaism—with all the diverse groups vying within the vague mainstream and sometimes on its edges— should one locate Jesus the Jew?

Not too long ago the stock answers would have been largely in terms of one of the groups mentioned by the first-century Jewish historian Josephus. Some scholars said that Jesus was a Pharisee in the mold of Hillel, because of his compassionate and humane approach to the Mosaic Law. No, said others, Jesus was a Pharisee in the mold of Shammai, because of his stringent view of the grounds for divorce. No, said others, Jesus was a Pharisee who mixed the approaches of Hillel and Shammai. No, said others, Jesus was a Sadducee, because he rejected the whole idea of a normative oral tradition as espoused by the Pharisees. No, said others, Jesus was an Essene, because he shared their rejection of the Jerusalem temple as then constituted and because he shared their belief in an imminent future victory of God over the forces of evil.

However, the work of scholars like Dr. Cohen, in his book *From the Maccabees to the Mishnah*, has reminded us that many Palestinian Jews at the turn of the era felt no obligation to belong to any of these groups. Moreover, the great variety of works at

Qumran suggests that there may have been other Jewish groups active in the period about whom we know very little or nothing.

Then, too, there were special, striking individuals whose practice and message simply refused pigeonholing and whose conscious choices moved them to the margins of the mainstream. John the Baptist comes readily to mind, as well as the ascetic Jew named Bannus, who acted as a guru for Josephus during his teenage years. John the Baptist, Bannus, and some other Jews of the period present us with individual Jewish religious figures who belonged to no one discernible group. More to the point, because of their special, at times strange, teachings or mode of life, which they freely chose, they were atypical, "ab-normal" in the root sense of the word, "marginal" in that they deviated from the ordinary life and practice of most Palestinian Jews.

It is within this vague category of "marginal Jew" that I have tentatively placed Jesus of Nazareth. Hence the title of my work, *A Marginal Jew*.[3] I must emphasize here that, in using the word "marginal," I am *not* in any way denying or watering down the Jewishness of Jesus. In many ways, Jesus shared in the broad mainstream of Judaism already described. Indeed, in some ways, for example in rejecting a starkly ascetic lifestyle in the desert, he was less marginal than John the Baptist or Bannus. I emphasize, therefore, that I fully accept the Jewishness of Jesus as I try to locate him more precisely on the map of first-century Judaism by examining the ways in which he was atypical, abnormal, or marginal *within*, not *outside of*, Judaism. My approach must be understood as complementary, not contradictory, to that of Dr. Cohen.

One common approach to the question of the "difference"— some would say "uniqueness"—of Jesus within Judaism is to focus on the particular moral, ethical, and legal questions—the *halakhot*—in which Jesus notably differed from most Jews of his day. For example, although one can debate the historicity of individual sayings of Jesus in the Gospels almost endlessly, there seems to be a fair consensus that the historical Jesus rejected divorce absolutely for his followers. In this he seems to have gone beyond

---

[3] John P. Meier, *A Marginal Jew: Rethinking the Historical Jesus*, vol. I: *The Roots of the Problem and the Person*, and vol. II: *Mentor, Message, Miracles* (New York: Doubleday, 1991, 1994).

even the stringency of the Essenes, certainly beyond the views of other Jewish groups of the time. He also seems to have rejected totally the use of oaths and vows. Some scholars would also maintain that Jesus rejected any form of legal retaliation. Much more debatable is the question of whether a saying rejecting the kosher food laws (Mark 7:15–19) goes back to Jesus. Some critics defend its authenticity, while others attribute the saying to the early church. To these unusual teachings one could add the striking differences in Jesus' "lifestyle." As far as we can tell, he chose to remain celibate, a highly unusual but not entirely unknown status in Judaism at the time.[4] He rejected the practice of voluntary fasting for his disciples, and presumably for himself.

Now, one could easily continue down this road of listing individual points of teaching or practice in which Jesus differed from most Jews of his day. In each case one could argue the question first of the historicity of the saying or story in the Gospels and then of the difference in Jesus' practice—be it real or imagined— from that of "mainstream" Judaism. However, by the time I finished writing Volume Two of *A Marginal Jew* about a month ago, I had come to question whether this was the most profitable way of approaching the problem of Jesus' difference or uniqueness within Judaism. While these individual points of difference may be important, I think it is vital to try to grasp, in at least some inchoate and tentative way, the overall convergence, configuration, or *Gestalt* of Jesus' teachings and practice—that overall configuration which made him a different kind of Jew within first-century Palestinian Judaism.

I would suggest three major components that help constitute the unusual configuration of Jesus as a marginal Jew:

(1) At the very least, in some vague sense Jesus was seen by others and by himself as an eschatological prophet, perhaps *the* eschatological prophet, that is, the last divinely inspired messenger sent-by God to his people Israel in the last days. For Jesus proclaimed the imminent coming of God's kingly rule and reign ("the kingdom of God"), a strange message made stranger by the strange messenger, an itinerant celibate layman.

(2) Yet, unlike John the Baptist, Jesus proclaimed and cele-

---

[4] On this see Meier, *A Marginal Jew*, vol. I, pp. 332–45.

brated the kingdom of God not only imminent in the future but already present in his ministry. It was present in his powerful preaching and teaching, present in his table fellowship offered to all, including toll collectors and sinners. But most strikingly the kingdom of God was present, palpable, and effective for Jesus' Jewish audience in certain striking, astounding deeds—deeds that Jesus' followers, and at least some of his foes, considered miracles. I stress here that I am not claiming that Jesus actually performed miracles. That is ultimately a theological, not an historical judgment. I am simply observing as an historian that various Jewish contemporaries, from Jesus' disciples through his adversaries to Josephus, *thought* that he performed miracles and that Jesus himself *claimed* to do so. In Volume Two of *A Marginal Jew*, I maintain that the belief that Jesus performed exorcisms, healed the sick, and in a few instances even raised the dead to life actually goes back to the ministry of Jesus and is not simply a product of the early church.

(3) These supposed miracles, especially the supposed miracles of raising the dead, would almost inevitably cast Jesus in the role of Elijah or Elisha, the only prophets of ancient Israel who were believed to have performed a whole string of miracles, including raising the dead. Jesus' status as an itinerant prophet as well as a miracle worker, a prophet who operated particularly in northern Israel, a prophet who spoke rather than wrote, a prophet who called disciples—all these elements would make the fit between himself on the one hand and Elijah and Elisha on the other still closer.

An intriguing side-question arises here. Would Jesus' Jewish audience think of him more in terms of Elijah or of Elisha? From Malachi through Ben Sira to the New Testament and beyond into the rabbinic literature, Elijah was *the* eschatological prophet par excellence, the prophet whose return from heaven (whither he had been taken up in a fiery chariot) would signal the last days, the regathering and cleansing of Israel, the resolving of all legal questions, and the coming of God to rule in full power.[5] Hence

---

[5] See, e.g., Malachi 3:23–24 in the Masoretic Text (4:5–6 in English translations); Ben Sira 48:1–11; Luke 1:17; John 1:19–21; Mark 9:11–13; Revelations 11:3–6; *Mishnah Ed.* 8:7; *Mishnah Sota* 9:15. Later Jewish and Christian versions of an Apocalypse of Elijah, which may go back to a Jewish source written ca.

the eschatological prophet and miracle worker from Nazareth would naturally be connected with Elijah in particular rather than with Elisha. Whether people thought that Jesus was literally the returned Elijah or rather another prophet clothed with Elijah's mantle and fulfilling Elijah's role is the kind of abstruse question and fine distinction that probably did not trouble the minds of many of Jesus' followers.

Whatever his precise relation to the Elijah of old, Jesus the eschatological prophet was acting out the *role* of the eschatological Elijah as he both proclaimed the imminent coming of God's rule and made that rule a reality even now by his miracles. It was this convergence and configuration of different traits in the one man named Jesus—traits that made him the Elijah-like eschatological prophet of a kingdom both future and yet made present by his miracles—that gave Jesus his distinctiveness or "uniqueness" within Palestinian Judaism of the early first century.[6]

All this stands in stark contrast to one portrait of the historical Jesus sometimes found in popular literature today: Jesus was a kind-hearted rabbi who preached gentleness and love in the spirit of Hillel. This domestication of a strange first-century marginal Jew bears a curious resemblance to the domestication of Jesus undertaken by Thomas Jefferson some two centuries ago. The advantage and appeal of the domesticated Jesus are obvious: he is instantly relevant to and usable by contemporary ethics, homilies,

---

100 C.E., expanded and varied Elijah's connection to and role in the end-time events. On this see Orval S. Wintermute, "Elijah, Apocalypse of," *Anchor Bible Dictionary*, 2, pp. 466–69.

[6] Here in particular one might be tempted to construct a grand "developmental" theory embracing both John the Baptist and Jesus. John prophesied the imminent arrival of the eschatological figure whom he called "the one who comes." In keeping with some strains of Jewish eschatology at the time, John may have used this mysterious phrase "the one who comes" as a cryptic description of Elijah, the last human precursor of God himself. During his time in John's circle of disciples, Jesus would have grown used to such an expectation. When he began his own eschatological ministry, and especially when he discovered his power to perform Elijah-like miracles, Jesus would have come to see himself as the Elijah whose coming John had promised. Like so many developmental theories, this one is both engaging and unprovable. Throughout the volumes of *A Marginal Jew*, I purposely eschew any highly speculative theory that "explains it all" in favor of a judicious weighing of evidence in order to arrive at modest but fairly secure conclusions about what the historical Jesus did and said.

political programs, and ideologies of various stripes. In contrast, a first-century Jew who presents himself as the eschatological prophet of the imminent arrival of God's kingdom, a kingdom that the prophet makes present and effective by his Elijah-like miracles, is not so instantly relevant and usable. Yet, for better or for worse, this strange marginal Jew, this eschatological prophet and miracle worker, *is* the historical Jesus retrievable by modern historical methods applied soberly to the data. His one advantage is that he need not fear losing his instant relevance in the eyes of intellectuals, since he has none to begin with.

Still, this is not the whole story, the entire configuration. To these three major components one must add a fourth component, one I have already mentioned, namely, Jesus' unusual moral and legal teaching. Besides being the eschatological prophet and miracle worker clothed in the aura of Elijah, Jesus not only taught his Jewish followers general ethical imperatives (e.g., love and forgiveness) but also presumed to give concrete directions on how to observe the Mosaic Law (*halakhot*). Some of his pronouncements on the Mosaic Law led to disputes with other Jewish groups, and not without reason. Apparently at times Jesus, while certainly affirming the Law as God's word to Israel, took it upon himself to rescind or change some individual institutions in the Law: e.g., divorce, oaths and vows, and, in the opinion of some scholars, even the kosher food laws of the Torah. This element of concrete-and controversial directives as well as general teaching on the Law added further spicy ingredients to an already heady brew. In sum: Jesus not only presented himself as the eschatological prophet of the coming kingdom of God, not only presented himself as the Elijah-like miracle worker who made the future kingdom already effective and palpable to his followers, but at the same time presented himself as a teacher who could tell Israelites how to observe the Law of Moses—indeed, who could even tell Israelites what they should or should not observe in the Law.

Thus, what some have called the "charismatic" nature of Jesus, already discernible in his prophetic ministry and miracle working, also surfaces in his teaching on the Law. As a true charismatic, Jesus located the source of his authority not in recognized traditional channels of authority (e.g., the Law and the accepted modes of interpreting it, the rulings of priests or authoritative courts, or the sayings of famous teachers) but rather in his own ability to know directly and intuitively what was God's will for his people Israel in the last days. In the end, this is just another aspect of Jesus' implicit claim to be the charismatic prophet of the end time, a claim that extended from strictly prophetic and miraculous activity into the more scribal activity of interpreting the Law and guiding concrete behavior. At this point, the convergence and configuration of multiple roles in the one man called Jesus become extremely dense and complicated.

In my view, that is all to the good. For, if we are to speak at all of the "uniqueness" of Jesus the Jew—and the term uniqueness is questionable—the uniqueness should be located not in this or that teaching, in this or that action, but rather in the total configuration I have just sketched. I would suggest that perhaps it is by exploring this configuration of an atypical, abnormal, or marginal Jew within the broader context of mainstream Palestinian Judaism in the first century that Jewish and Christian scholars might find new paths toward fruitful dialogue, mutual understanding, and the promotion of mutual respect among their respective communities. It is with this hope that I offer my reflections this evening as we seek to celebrate and foster the humane and enlightened views expressed in *Nostra Aetate*.

Shaye J. D. Cohen: Thank you. My talk tonight is in three parts: First: was Jesus Jewish? Second: how Jewish was he? Third: what are the implications of his Jewishness? The answer to the first question is simple. I do not have to expand upon what Peter Steinfels just said. Jesus was born a Jew, lived a Jew, etc. He was clearly and thoroughly Jewish and there is no reason to assume anything to the contrary. So the question would seem rather open and shut.

There is a later tradition told in some circles of the church that Paul, who claims in his own words to be a Jew born and bred, in reality was born a gentile and converted to Judaism. There is such a tradition later in the church but, as far as I know, there is no such tradition about Jesus told by anybody. There was a great deal of discussion then and now about Jesus' paternity and maternity. As we all know, if you want to know if somebody is Jewish, the first thing you are supposed to ask is, who is the mother? Jesus' mother is a relatively simple question. All accounts agree on her identity, and she clearly was a Jewish woman. Ergo Jesus himself will have been a Jew. The identity of Jesus' father is a different question entirely.

There is an anti-Christian tradition, apparently of Jewish origin, that Jesus' father was a Roman soldier named Panthera (or Pandira—the name is spelled in different ways). This is clearly meant to be a hostile retelling of the virgin birth story of the Gospels. In his book, Fr. Meier writes that this tradition does not predate the second century of our era. He may be right but I do not know. In any case that is the closest that anybody in antiquity came to suggesting that Jesus was not born a Jew.

In modern times there has been a movement among some Christians, which I believe does not antedate the latter part of the nineteenth century, to try to limit or minimize as much as possible Jesus' Jewishness. This movement began in Germany, of course, and argued that the Galileans were primarily a gentile population forcibly Judaized by the Hasmoneans, and that this Judaization was incomplete and only surface deep. The ethnic stock was primarily gentile. Jesus derives from Galilean stock. Therefore he is ethnically of non-Jewish stock. This theory is clearly an attempt made by people under the influence of racial anti-Semitism to do their best to de-Judaize Christianity, to remove the Jewish roots of Christianity. These attempts culminate of course in the Nazi group called the *Deutsche Christen* who systematically did their best to de-Judaize Christianity, even so much as throwing out Paul to a great degree. All of this is a very interesting phenomenon, the subject of a forthcoming monograph by Susannah Heschel, but I think it is clearly irrelevant to a student of first-century Judaism.

What is even more remarkable is that Jewish sources themselves do not have any hesitation as regarding Jesus as a Jew. You might have thought that at some point the Jews would have written him off and thought of him as a gentile. But no, even Jewish sources as far as I know consistently look at Jesus as a Jew: a wayward Jew, of course; a bad Jew, of course; a heretic, of course, a magician, a deceiver, an idolater, an adulterer—all that is, of course, true. But in the final analysis, Jesus was a Jew and consequently someone who was punished by the Jewish authorities because, as a Jew, he was liable to punishment by them. In the nineteenth century many Jews began to claim that Jesus was not a bad Jew but a good Jew, a viewpoint that clearly reflects the emancipation of the Jews and their integration into European society. But that is another lecture.

One final point. There is no evidence anywhere in the Gospels, as far as I can see (and I will happily yield to Fr. Meier if he thinks I am wrong), that Jesus intended to found a new religion, or saw himself as a founder of a new religion, or was seen by others as a founder of a new religion. Even the Gospel writers, even in the latest or redactional layers of the Gospels, leave us with little evidence that at this stage of the Christian tradition Jesus was understood as the founder of a new religion. The only possible evidence to the contrary is the parable of the vineyard (Matthew 21:33–46 and parallels), a very striking text, in which the owner of a vineyard (= God) puts his tenants to death because of their maltreatment of his servants (= prophets) and his son (= Jesus), and brings in new tenants who will work the vineyard properly. This can be read as a parable talking about God's rejection of the Jews and the introduction of a new Israel—indeed, the church fathers regularly read the parable this way. But the next verse says quite clearly that the villains of the piece, the old tenants, are not the Jews in general but the high priests and the Pharisees (Matthew 21:45). So even here, where we come closest to finding a supersessionist theology (a theology which has Christianity supersede or replace Judaism), we do not really see it. The Gospels themselves do not advance that position. In the Gospels, Jesus was a Jew who remained a Jew and did nothing to establish a new religion.

So now to my second question: what kind of Jew was he? It is clear on all accounts that Jesus was an unusual Jew, a Jew who left a strong impression on those who met him. The Gospel accounts are filled with stories about people being "amazed" by something that Jesus said or did. They were truly moved. He was a man of commanding presence, clearly a person who was not easily forgotten. Indeed, Jesus' entire career is unusual. How many Jewish boys from a small town in Galilee teach with authority, debate the Pharisees, Scribes, and high priests, and get handed over to the Romans to be crucified? That is not your typical career for a nice Jewish boy. We are dealing with someone who by any definition is unusual. In his lecture Fr. Meier discusses more of these qualities that made Jesus unusual and set him apart from his Jewish context.

I would like to focus briefly on some qualities that made him a typical Jew, or at least a Jew well within a normal pattern or range of Jewish behavior. What do we see as we read the Gospel account as a whole? We see Jesus saying and doing many things that we may presume were fairly typical for Jews in the first century of our era. For example, he goes to synagogue. He reads the scriptures in the synagogue. He endorses the temple rituals (recall the healing of the leper, Matthew 8:1–4 and parallels), and participates in the paschal (Passover) sacrifice. Clearly he has a strong belief in our Father in heaven, not only belief in God, as I am sure all Jews had, but a sense of the divine presence as real, immediate, and palpable and not something philosophical or a product of ratiocination.

All this, we may assume, was typical for many Jews in antiquity: a strong desire to want to please God; a strong desire to do that which God wants, to understand scripture properly, to observe the commandments properly. People are asking him, what is the greatest commandment? What does God want me to do? Everybody in that society wants to please God, to observe the commandments, to understand the Torah and the scriptures properly. In that sense he fits right into what I assume is typical of his culture.

Similarly, Jesus seems to have had a clear sense of otherness vis-à-vis gentiles. He shares the Jewish sense that the world consists of two kinds of people: us and them. He directs his activities to Jews, and talks about Jews. When the Canaanite woman brings her daughter to him to be healed, he is not sure how to deal with her; "I was sent only to the lost sheep of the house of Israel" is his reply (Matthew 15:21–28 and parallels). There are very few incidents, in fact, in which Jesus is reported to have dealt with non-Jews. This suggests that Jesus shared the world view and the Jewish identity that were common among the Jews of the first century. They regarded themselves as Jews, as distinct from the rest of humanity.

Perhaps most controversial is Jesus' observance of the Jewish laws. He makes disparaging comments about the laws, but it is always the disciples, not Jesus himself, who are reported to be breaking the laws. His disciples pluck grain on the Sabbath. His disciples do not fast. His disciples eat with unwashed hands. What of Jesus himself? The most heinous violation he is reported to have committed is that he heals people on the Sabbath. I am not sure if this is truly a violation of the Sabbath or not; if it is, it is a violation of a technicality. Perhaps his disciples violated the traditional laws because they thought that they derived authority to do so from him. Jesus certainly excuses their conduct when questioned about it. Still, given the fact that observance of the laws of the "Old Testament" (if I may use a Christian term) was such an important and contentious issue in early Christianity, I am struck by the failure of the authors of the Gospels to have remembered, or invented, stories demonstrating Jesus' violation of the Jewish laws. I deduce that Jesus the Jew adhered to the legal norms of the Jewish community, in spite of his run-ins with various authority figures and in spite of his polemics against them.

In some respects Jesus typifies not the average Jew on the street but the virtuoso Jew, the Jew who had a secure place in Jewish society but who was far from average or "normal." Jesus was a preacher and a teacher; not every Jew was (or is) a preacher and a teacher. He was also a healer, or, as my teacher Morton Smith liked to call him, a magician. He was also a prophet, or at least was widely regarded as a prophet. This is clearly a note of distinction, since not every Jew walking on the streets of Galilee or Jerusalem in the first century performed magical acts of healing or combined healing with prophetic inspiration. Still, these are all recognized social types. We know of many other preachers, teachers, healers, magic men, prophets, and holy men in the first century of our era.

Jesus attracted disciples and created a group of disciples who saw their bonds to him as surpassing their bonds to their families. This too is a well-known social phenomenon, which may be called sectarian formation or school formation. The first century of our era was the age of sects or schools among the Jews of Judaea. The best known, of course, are the Pharisees, Sadducees, Essenes (who seem to have been identical with the Qumran sect), Zealots, and Sicarii, but we may be sure that there were others, in addition to the early Christians. Not all Jews were members of one of these schools or sects—on the contrary, it seems likely that the vast majority belonged to no school or sect at all—but the early Jesus movement had its place, and its parallels, within Jewish society of the period.

Last, Jesus seems to have been animated by a pietistic streak which we can find elsewhere in ancient Judaism. According to him, even having adulterous thoughts is adultery—this is an extreme pietism. He attacks the temple, he attacks Jewish authority figures, he attacks the priests. The Qumran scrolls show us another pietistic group attacking the Jewish authorities, especially the temple priests, for being lax, tolerant, corrupt, immoral, impure, unjust, and so on. Jesus' arguments with the Pharisees, priests, scribes, and elders, and his prophecy of the destruction of the temple, are sometimes taken as evidence for his distance from Judaism, but the opposite seems to have been the case. His critique is the critique not of a would-be outsider but of a would-be insider. He is alienated from the institutions of society but he hopes that the institutions of society will reform themselves in directions of which he would approve. If they do not, he, like the Jews of Qumran, is confident that they will be removed by God and replaced by newer ones that will be more just and more righteous. (This seems to be the point of the parable of the vineyard, which I mentioned above.) This critique of the central institutions of Jewish society is part of Jesus' Jewishness, and is amply paralleled elsewhere in Jewish society.

Now I turn to my third question: so what? I have argued that for the most part Jesus' behavior was well within the norms of Jewish society. He was not a typical Jew, but he was distinctive in ways that also made other Jews and other Jewish groups distinctive. If this view is correct, so what? In the old days the fact that Jesus was Jewish meant that the religion which he founded, or was thought to have founded, must be a new Judaism to replace the old Judaism. If he was Jewish, then he must have taken Judaism along with him on his way to establishing Christianity. Judaism, in Christian eyes, was left without reason or purpose, without validity or authority. Christians claimed the patriarchs, the covenant, the Bible, the title "Israel," and indeed all of biblical history, as their own. As a church writer of the second century says in his dialogue with a Jew, the Scriptures are "not yours but ours" (Justin Martyr, *Dialogue with Trypho*, 29). Jews and Christians argued over who was the true Israel, as if there were not enough theological truth to go around. Therefore each side saw truth in exclusive terms, and each side claimed it for itself. In Christian eyes Jesus the Jew signified the end of Judaism; in Jewish eyes Jesus the Jew signified a rebellion against all that was sacred and true.

In our pluralistic world, we realize that theology of this sort is inadequate and can often lead to deleterious consequences that are painfully obvious to us all. We realize that we must now seek to develop non-exclusive claims to truth, a position which has no warrant in either the Jewish or Christian traditions, and represents a clear break with the past.

The challenge that the Jewishness of Jesus brings to Christianity is that Christians must develop a non-supersessionist theology, a theology that validates the Christian message and the Christian promise without at the same time de-legitimating Judaism *for Jews*. Christians must find a way to maintain Christianity's identity and sense of purpose without at the same time denying Judaism a reason for its continued existence. That is a contemporary challenge to those who take seriously Jesus' Jewishness.

The challenge that the Jewishness of Jesus brings to Judaism is that Jews must develop a theology of the Other, a theology that validates the Jewish way without at the same time de-legitimating the Christian message and the Christian promise *for Christians*. We Jews must realize that Christians, too, have a claim to the Old Testament (as the Christians call it) and to biblical history, and that the Christian claims are no less real and no less authentic than our own. The challenge is to recognize that Christianity, too, is (or at least once was) a form of Judaism, and we Jews must work out in our own minds a way of understanding what Christianity is, and what purpose Christianity serves in the cosmic order. As far as I know Jewish thinkers have barely begun to confront this challenge, but the challenge must be confronted.

Peter Steinfels: Let us take the occasion for comments from each of you to the other about your two presentations.

Shaye Cohen: I have two brief comments. First, I have always been struck by the continued reference of Jesus to God as "my Father" or "my Father in heaven," in the first person singular. Of course Jewish liturgy traditionally refers to God as Father, but I am pressed to find another Jew in the first century who routinely refers to God as "my Father." It would be as if someone today would refer to God as "dad," which would strike us as very strange. Yes, God is "our Father," but he is not dad. I do not know where the tradition comes from but it strikes me as really odd. Is this part of your charismatic traditions, the palpable sense of God's reality and nearness, the kingdom of heaven tradition? But why is this usage attested nowhere else?

A second question, perhaps related to the first. I agree with you that Jesus sets himself up as an authority counter to the Torah: "You have heard it said but I say it to you." But if we are honest we must admit, of course, that the rabbis do the same thing on every single page of rabbinical literature. They routinely distort and turn upside down the meaning of the biblical texts they are discussing. The difference between them, of course, is that the rabbis pretend that they are not doing it while Jesus admits that he is, in fact, proposing an alternative system of morality superseding that of the original text. Jesus has a kind of historical awareness of the distance between Moses and himself, while the rabbis do not. Is this the difference? Or is there something more substantial? Those will be my two questions to you.

John Meier: I purposely tried to avoid this evening all those questions which would usually come under the heading of a historical Jesus leading us to Christology, namely, all the various titles used of Jesus in the Gospels, and even the question of his calling God "Father." That leads down so many circuitous alleys, and also that is going to be part of the material treated in my volume three. In writing *A Marginal Jew*, I have made a firm rule which I find useful: never to try to pose a question to myself until I have to write the chapter dealing with that issue. When I write, I find myself going into the chapter with one point of view and being lurched around 180 degrees by the time I come out of the chapter. I have made a point of not making any decisions before getting to that point of the book.

I will try to answer Dr. Cohen's question very briefly. The "Father" question is a difficult one. On the one hand, I would say there is a massive increase of "Father" language in the later Gospels of Matthew and John, and I think that is to be put down to both the traditions and the final redactional work of those two streams of the Gospels. On the other hand, however, using the criterion of multiple attestation of sources, the fact is that "Father" language is so widespread throughout the various streams of the Gospel tradition that I think we can safely say that this was a striking way of speaking about God, used by the historical Jesus, which, like many things, "sold like crazy"—for example, the use of "Amen" at the beginning of a statement and the "Amen I say to you." That seems to be from Jesus, but Matthew goes whole hog with it and John thought it was so good it became "Amen, Amen I say to you." If it is good once, it is better twice.

So I would say that, indeed, there is something there with the historical Jesus. It is striking that the different traditions, without the ability to cross-check one another, or control one another, constantly, automatically, and without reflecting upon it, made the distinction between Jesus speaking about "my Father" and Jesus speaking to the disciples about "your Father" and telling them to pray either "Father" or "our Father." But he never puts himself with them under the common rubric of "our Father." There is something intriguing there.

There is also the difficult question of the use of *Abba*, which was perhaps overplayed by Joachim Jeremias.[7] As a result, vast numbers of Catholics are drowning in *Abba* piety at the moment. All the soupy piety we used to have with Mary and Jesus we now have with *Abba*. It is the Aramaic revenge of the Gospels. It is useful to realize that basically we have three occurrences of *Abba* in the New Testament. Two are by Paul in Galatians and Romans, talking about how Christians pray. One and only one time do we have Jesus speaking *Abba*, but that is in Gethsemane when supposedly nobody else is around. So how did anybody know that he used it?

Actually, I think that one can make a good argument that this usage does go back to Jesus himself. It is a rather peculiar usage in

---

[7] Joachim Jeremias, *The Prayers of Jesus* (Napierville, Ill.: A. R. Allenson, 1967).

direct prayer to God. To answer Shaye's questions I think, yes, there seems to be something here in this charismatic connection, Jesus does seem to be claiming some special sort of relationship with God, which however I think cannot be defined further simply on the basis of his use of Father or *Abba*. I think that has been pushed much too far . A whole Christology is created out of one word. All I think we can say is, yes it does seem to go back to Jesus and does seem to indicate his expression of some very particular personal relationship.

Secondly, as for the question of Torah, I think there is a real problem determining which of those sayings actually go back to Jesus. For instance, I have now come reluctantly to the view that the whole "it was said to the men of old but I say to you" may not come from Jesus at all. That may indeed be Matthean tradition and redaction; it is peculiarly Matthean. However, the very firm "Amen I say to you," with some sort of pronouncement following, does seem to go back to Jesus himself. I would see Jesus affirming the Torah as God's will for Israel, but, as in all things, the end time brings to perfection and conclusion what was present in perhaps an incomplete and not completely understood way. Of course, legal authorities through the whole of history, while affirming total obedience to constitution and law, constantly undo, rewrite, and change the intention of the original.

Dr. Cohen points out very well that perhaps the difference with Jesus is the chutzpah of saying "yes, I am going to do it," "I am going to flaunt it." I think the reason for the flaunting is connected with the sense of the end time: that what was present in Israel in perhaps somewhat of a fragmentary or not completely understood way is now being brought to completion and perfection in the end time, and as a result you have to fasten a few screws here, loosen a few things there, and rearrange deck chairs a little bit. I would maintain that basic fidelity to Torah and yet some changes in Torah are part of this general eschatological consciousness.

As for the question of the New Testament authors vis-à-vis Jesus, I would have no problem at all saying that Jesus did not intend to found a new religion. As Gerhard Lofink put it very well, how could Jesus intend to found a church when he found a church already waiting for him on the scene, namely the *Qahal*, the Knesset of Israel? That was the church. Again, there might be a question of eschatological fulfillment, but the church of God was already there. There was no need found a church. There was a church. It was called Israel.

While that is firmly the idea of Jesus, the problem is that the New Testament shows the same sort of pluralism vis-à-vis Israel that it shows toward Christology, that it shows toward morality and everything else. Therefore, it seems to me that in the case of Matthew, John, and the Epistle of the Hebrews, there may be some sense of break and change, some sense of a different people that has arisen, at least in the minds of the evangelists. Would you be willing to make a distinction, within the New Testament works, between those which certainly do not have supersessionism and those which at least might have an opening toward supersessionism?

Shaye Cohen: Yes, I certainly agree. I do not consider myself an expert student of the New Testament, but my impression as a reader is that one can hear different voices speaking. It is a polyphonic text. John obviously stands apart, even to a casual reader. John's repeated reference to "the Jews" is very striking, as is Jesus' constant distancing of himself from "the Jews." It is clear that something dramatic has happened in the social setting behind this document compared to the social setting behind the other three Gospels. Matthew is both closer to Judaism and further from Judaism than Mark and Luke. He seems to know more about Jews, Jewish things, and Jewish beliefs, than anybody else. Yet he is also the one with the most virulent rejection of the Jewish leaders, as in the parable of the vineyard (Matthew 21:33–46 and parallels) and the denunciation of the Pharisees (Matthew 23). So yes, I agree with you that there is a polyphony here. The question, of course, for Christian theologians is: Which themes do we listen to, or which ones do we take seriously? But it is not my job to tell Catholics what to do. I can give advice and suggestions, but after that point I simply withdraw.

John Meier: You mentioned in your talk about the many miracle workers at the time of Jesus. As I was going through the miracle traditions, what struck me was that when one tries to name other miracle workers, usually the people named are identified as miracle workers in the later rabbinic tradition, but it is very difficult to establish that tradition for the early first century: only Hanina, and a few other people. They seem to become miracle workers more and more as we go further into rabbinic tradition. But I had trouble finding people I could name in early first-century Palestine who actually were miracle workers, as opposed to Josephus' sign prophets. They are people who promised a great act of deliverance, but you do not see them going around performing miracles as they are trying to gather disciples. What would be your thoughts on that?

Shaye Cohen: That is a good distinction which I had not thought of; please allow me to think while I stand on one foot (as the rabbinic proverb has it). The rabbinic tradition about miracle figures does grow and change, as you mention. But that there is a miracle tradition is clear, I think, even in the earliest texts. Once again, I would not want to defend the historicity of any of the stories told about any of these figures any more than I would want to defend the historicity of any of the stories told about Jesus. We are dealing with figures who are remembered in a very peculiar way. They are not remembered as legal authorities. They are remembered as magicians, magic men, or holy men. The tradition comes from somewhere. Similarly Josephus, as I recall, has stories not only about sign prophets, but also about healers; he tells of one Eleazar who used plant roots and incantations prescribed by Solomon in order to expel demons (*Jewish Antiquities* 8.2.5 46–48). Of course you also have Simon Magus (Acts 8).

Peter Steinfels: Despite some timidity instilled by this dazzling display up here, I suspect that many of you are ready to pose your own questions to our speakers and this is your opportunity.

Audience member: Professor Meier, many years ago at the age of sixteen I came to the independent conclusion that Christianity was misnamed and it should be called Paulinity. Very recently, in of all places the *Wall Street Journal*, I read a book review about anti-Semitism which very broadly said that Paul was the first ant-Semite and that it was done for political reasons to get himself in better with the Romans. Do you think it is any help in tonight's discussion about the Judaism of Jesus to perhaps label Paul as the first Christian?

John Meier: I am afraid I am about to say something that may be shocking to some, but I think perhaps it is best to get this out right away. Paul is greatly overrated. Christianity began before Paul, was going on alongside of Paul, and would have continued without Paul. Paul helped it very greatly, but the idea that Paul was pivotal in Christianity is one of the most overblown ideas that you usually find in New Testament courses. He did, of course, have a great impact on Christianity; but Christianity was already there before him, Christianity formed him as well as being formed by him, and there were plenty of other streams of Christianity alongside of him that either put up with him or despised him. We must exorcise from our conceptions of Christian origins the idea that somehow everything either began with Paul or depended upon Paul. As far as we can tell—and granted it is disputable—Matthew, Mark, and John all wrote their expressions of the Christianity of their churches without knowing Paul or presenting a theology that was Pauline. The same is true of the other major epistolary traditions in the New Testament, apart from First and Second Peter, and certainly the Revelation of John does not display a knowledge of Paul. There are whole streams and blocks of the New Testament that knew nothing about Paul—or cared nothing about Paul if they knew about him—and went merrily on their own way, to say nothing, of course, of the Epistle of James. Hence, I think the answer to your question is obvious. To call Paul the first Christian is to mistake one stream of the tradition for the whole tradition, which was much vaster than the one man Paul.

Audience member: I have two questions. What was the distance in time between Jesus and the Gospel writers? What did Jesus mean by "the Kingdom of God is within me?"

John Meier: Obviously, dating is always a tricky business. One of the last books of J. A. T. Robinson was *Redating the New Testament* (Philadelphia: Westminster, 1976), in which he tried to show that the whole of the New Testament was written before 70 of the common era. Everybody thought it was ridiculous. The common opinion is that Jesus came upon the scene in his public ministry somewhere about the year 28 of the common era, give or take a few years, and that he died somewhere between 30 and 33—again, give or take a few years. The general opinion is that the first Gospel to be written was the Gospel of Mark, somewhere around the year 70. Again I say "general opinion" because not all would agree with it. Matthew's Gospel probably was written somewhere around 85. John's Gospel probably went through a number of editions somewhere between 90 to 100. Interestingly, the first scrap of papyrus of the Gospels that we have is from John's Gospel, one of the latest if not *the* latest to be written; the papyrus scrap is usually dated around the year 125 to 130 C.E. in Egypt. Strangely, one of the last Gospels to be written is the first one of which we have a scrap—to be precise, from Chapter 18 of John's Gospel.

Luke is, for me, the wild card. I do not know when Luke was written. Fr. Fitzmyer, who has written a two-volume commentary on Luke, wants to put him somewhere after 70 but before 90 or so.[8] Other people want to put him very close to the end of the century. Still other people have pushed him into the early second century. I tend to think Luke was written toward the end of the century. You can see, obviously, that there is a lengthy development in the growth of the Gospel tradition.

To answer your second question about the Kingdom of God, the Greek preposition *entos* is properly translated "the Kingdom of God is *in your midst*" (Luke 17:21). An interiorizing, spiritualizing tendency tries instead to understand that the Kingdom of God is *within* you, as some sort of interior, spiritual thing. While I think that is possible, I think it is an unlikely translation in this context. I think in the context, in a statement in Luke's Gospel, that the preposition *entos* actually means that the Kingdom of God is in your midst and yet you do not recognize it.

Audience member: Dr. Cohen, what is the relationship of Jesus and the Zealots?

---

[8] Joseph A. Fitzmyer, *The Gospel According to Luke*, 2 vols. (Garden City: Doubleday, 1981 and 1985).

Shaye Cohen: In the 1960s, a revolutionary age, it was a commonly argued that Jesus was somehow a revolutionary leader on the model of Daniel Cohn Bendit or Mark Rudd. The argument was based on the assumption that if you scratch the skin of any pious Jew in the first century, you would find an anti-Roman revolutionary. The name Iscariot was taken to mean "Sicarius." The most famous exposition of this thesis, at least in English, was S. G. F. Brandon's *Jesus and the Zealots* (Manchester: Manchester University Press, 1967), but there were many other treatments as well. The 1960s have come and gone, and that view has gone with it. I do not know of anyone who takes that view seriously any longer. It is amusing to see how long it lasted—but that is true of most things from the 1960s.

The best evidence for this view is the crucifixion. What is the charge on which Jesus is brought up before the authorities? Is it a political charge or not? Perhaps lurking behind the tradition that Jesus was crucified as "King of the Jews," there is reference to the fact that he may have been seen, at least by some people, as an agitator or revolutionary, whether or not he was one in fact. I would not go further than that.

Audience member: To Fr. Meier I would ask of your view of Jesus as a marginal Jew, what is the "so what" for the twentieth-century ecumenism? To Dr. Cohen I would ask, since you made quite explicit what the "so what" is in twentieth century ecumenism, are you a little worried that your picture of Jesus seems an awful lot like a late twentieth-century conservative rabbi?

John Meier: Shaye can think about it for awhile. I say at the beginning of Volume I, in a section called "a marginal note on marginality," that I pick the word "marginal" precisely as a tease word, as a parable and question more than as an answer. That is one way of beginning to wade through all this material with something that I see as a sort of *basso continuo* and a thread running through the whole. I tell you this quite honestly. I do not know where this is leading. I chose that as a way to go, as one path, and certainly not the only path to follow as I started this pilgrimage, which is turning out to be much longer than I thought it was going to be. I am beginning to see a certain amount of light at the end of the tunnel, but I am not quite sure if it is a locomotive coming at me or not.

Shaye Cohen: I will answer for John since he refuses to answer. The answer is that Jesus as a marginal Jew has no relevance whatsoever for twentieth-century ecumenism. As far as the charge leveled against me, that I describe Jesus to make him resemble myself, it is not my fault if the resemblance it is true. The serious point of the question is that clearly we have to be wary of projecting back onto the historical figure of Jesus our own values and notions of what is good and what is bad, so that if we admire Jesus we project that which we think is good and if we do not admire him we project that which we think is bad. We need to avoid this, although this is impossible to do.

In the old days, we scholars claimed we were objective. We no longer make such arrogant claims, or at least at Brown we no longer make them. We all know that we are deeply prejudiced in all sorts of areas, both conscious and unconscious. No doubt my own make-up and defining characteristics have somehow influenced my judgment of what seems to me to be essential to the picture of Jesus. No doubt if I were left-handed instead of right-handed my picture would be different. In the final analysis, all we can do is to try be self-aware. We have no alternative. We have no neutral point where we can stand and with a fulcrum move the world. We try to remain aware of our own frailties and foibles as we make our way through the tradition.

Audience member: Professor Meier, are you trying to say that Jesus is outside Judaism?

John Meier: I see Jesus very much within, not outside of Judaism. Some people see first-century Judaism as so much in flux and so tumultuous that you cannot talk of Judaism in the singular. Dr. Neusner suggests speaking of Judaisms in the plural. Now, as I tried to indicate, I think that may be pushing things a little bit too far. The fact is that ancient authors themselves spoke of *Ioudaismos* ("Judaism") and *Ioudaios* ("Jewish") They presumed that these words meant something that would be relatively clear to people. As I said, although you cannot talk about a monolithic, normative, orthodox Judaism in the first century, there is this vague mainstream and I try to list the elements that make up that mainstream. In most, if not all of those elements, Jesus is part of that mainstream, however much he may be in tension with some aspects of it. Nevertheless, certain of the things he apparently consciously and freely and almost willfully chose to do seemed to push him to the margin or the edge of that mainstream. One thing I still have to try to find out is why. I do not think he was a jerk. I do not think he was totally oblivious to what he was doing. Why would he want to push himself consciously, both in practice and in teaching, to the edge or the margin of that mainstream. I do not have a full answer for you yet. To answer your question, in no way do I wish to intimate, by using the term "marginal," that Jesus was outside of Judaism.

Shaye Cohen: One of the points I intentionally omitted from my list of characteristics that I regard as common or normal was the imminent expectation of the end. I am not sure what to do with it and have changed my mind any number of times. On the one hand it is widely repeated that in the first century all Jews everywhere are sitting on the edge of their seats waiting for the final curtain to come up. The last act of the eschatological drama would unfold for them. So we are told. The evidence for this view, however, is not as clear as we would like and comes mostly from the New Testament itself. Clearly, the circles which produced this document saw Jesus as the Messiah and the inaugurator of the end time. Within these circles, these beliefs were common and powerful; were they also common and powerful outside these circles?

Josephus has nary a word on the subject. You would never know from reading Josephus that Judaean society was riven by eschatological expectations and speculations. In only one brief passage does he even imply that the revolutionaries who fought the Romans in 66–73 C.E. were animated by the belief that their struggle would result in the overthrow of the Roman empire and the establishment of a Judaean kingdom in its place. Josephus attributes the origins of the war to social and political factors, not speculations about the end time.

Last is a series of documents that modern scholars dub "apocalyptic." A few apocalyptic texts are preserved among the Qumran scrolls, but the majority have reached us via the Christian church. Many scholars, especially in the early part of this century, were convinced that these Christian works were really of Jewish origin, and that they represented "typical" or "normal" Jewish piety far better than did the works of the rabbis.

I am not convinced by these arguments. The degree of Jewishness of these texts remains the subject of ongoing debate, and, in any case, no matter how Jewish they may be, they can hardly be said to represent the Judaism of the average Jew on the street. They are all learned works, esoteric and difficult, the product of a self-selected elite. As for the average Galilean farmer, Judaean peasant, or Caesarean dockworker, let us be serious. Were they interested in learning about the mysteries of the end time, or in putting bread on the table? Were they interested in the details of the messianic revelation or in drinking wine at the end of the day at the local taverna?

It seems clear to me that the mass of people, then and now, have no patience or tolerance for flights of fantasy on these matters. Salvation, redemption, the end time—people may hold various beliefs about these things, of course, and these beliefs may be strongly felt, but do these beliefs necessarily affect their inner beings or their daily lives? When they go to work in the morning, do they say "I really must attain salvation today" or "Today I will hasten the arrival of the end time"? Not likely. I am still undecided on the connection between eschatological expectations and daily life.

Audience member: Fr. Meier, you have written off Paul for this evening and also said that supersessionism is out of bounds. Nevertheless, I will take a chance and put this question to you. Attempts to find a non-supersessionist theology depend on some words of Paul. I understand you are saying that Jesus himself was not supersessionist, but what about the Gospel writers?

John Meier: The reason I am leery about even using the word supersessionism, besides the fact that it does not occur in the New Testament, is that the New Testament positions on Israel are not only varied and change a great deal from book to book, but the individual writers at times seem in tension in their own minds. As Dr. Cohen pointed out, the place that we get the clearest sense of break is in John's Gospel. But it is in John's Gospel above all others that a foreigner, a Samaritan, says to Jesus, you are a Jew, and Jesus replies that salvation is from the Jews. Even in John there is this tension that is not totally resolved.

It is likewise in Matthew, which as Dr. Cohen pointed out very well, is in some ways the Gospel tradition most deeply steeped in Judaism. Yet in the next-to-last pericope in the Gospel, in response to the rumor that someone stole the body of Jesus from the tomb, Matthew, in one of his rare asides (Matthew 28:15), turns to the audience at the end of the story and says that this rumor has spread "*among Jews* down to this day."

If I am leery about talking about supersessionism, it is because it is extremely difficult to talk about even a single book of the New Testament in this regard, given that the authors themselves are still very much in tension within their own minds about this and have not worked it out completely.

Paul is all over the place with Israel, from the fiercest sort of polemics in parts of the First Thessalonians and Galatians to some great-hearted statements in certain parts of Romans 9–11. If I seem to be unwilling to talk about supersessionism, it is because it is an unhappy and inadequate term for a very complex situation in the New Testament.

Shaye Cohen: Again, it is not for me to tell Catholics what theology they should adopt, but I would give a different sort of answer entirely. One of the major effects of historical scholarship is to denature the authority of texts that are otherwise regarded as timeless and absolute. For the believer, the Gospel texts are absolute and authoritative documents that float in time and space, not anchored in any time or context, in which Jesus' timeless words speak to the Church then, now, and for always. For the historian, of course, the Gospel accounts come out of a specific historical context and are shaped by specific social, political, religious, and economic forces, as are all other human artifacts from cave paintings down to our own times.

If you accept the latter approach it means that the Gospels are indeed bound by their context. The Gospel attacks on the Phari-

sees, on the scribes, elders, high priests, and other Jewish authorities, the ejection of the tenants of the vineyard—all this is the fruit
of intra-Jewish sectarian debate and dispute. One group of Jews
is attacking another, vigorously denouncing the other as illegitimate. The Qumran Jews were doing precisely the same thing.
We do not regard the Qumran texts as an accurate description of
the piety of the temple priests, and as a historian I cannot believe
what the Gospels tell me about the Pharisees. The Gospels give
us a hostile, partisan, unsympathetic depiction of the Pharisees for
the sectarian needs of their audience. If you accept this, then lib-
eral-minded Catholics can explain that they do not believe everything the Gospels say because they understand why the Gospels
say what they say.

Audience member: How do our panelists believe that this evening's program will influence Jewish-Catholic relations?

John Meier: One of the reasons that I agreed to participate this
evening is that one way to get the whole thing started is precisely
with this topic. Therefore, the importance of this evening is that
it could provide a model for Catholic colleges and universities to
institute Jewish chairs within Catholic institutions. That would
be a very practical, happy, and ecumenical result of what we are
doing here this evening.

Shaye Cohen: I believe strongly in the power of ideas. They
shape how we think about the world and how we see ourselves
and those around us. A major problem in our own American
culture is the problem of the Other. We seem no longer able to
deal sympathetically with the other. There are so many Others
popping up around us, each one claiming justified or unjustified
grievances, that we need to learn how to seek common ground.
   I believe that in its modest way this evening's discussion will
contribute to the larger enterprise of promoting Jewish-Christian
understanding. If we understand Jesus better, then we have helped
Jews understand Christianity and Christians understand Judaism.
Will this reduce anti-Semitism or anti-Catholicism? Probably
not—at least, not immediately. But we must keep trying. As a

first-century Jew may or may not have said, the truth shall set you free.

Audience member: Is not the Old Testament's tradition of revelation one the central ideas to Judaism and Christianity? How does this relate to this evening's theme?

Shaye Cohen: Anybody who accepts the authority of the Hebrew scriptures is confronted by prophets, people who claim to speak with divine authority and with the divine voice. Jesus either saw himself, or was seen by others, as part of this tradition. Jesus asks his disciples "Who do men say that I am?" They replied, "Some say John the Baptist, others say Elijah, and others Jeremiah or one of the prophets" (Matthew 16:13–14 and parallels).

Jews and Christians share this common heritage, although Jews would say that prophesy ceased during the Persian period in the fourth century B.C.E., whereas Christians would insist that it did not cease until Jesus himself. For Jews, Jesus will be a person who is deluded into thinking he is a prophet, and for Christians, Jews are wrong in denying his prophetic status. There were many others in Jewish society who regarded themselves as prophets or were seen as prophets, and none of them commanded universal assent. Jesus is one such.

John Meier: Once again we have the problem of later categories imposed on earlier texts. The Old Testament contains many, various ways in which the ineffable and unknowable One himself, in some way, revealed himself and expressed his will to his people, Israel. Two key images of the way God reveals himself are God's word and God's spirit. It is not, therefore, by accident that the concepts of word and spirit are so abundant in the New Testament. For all the good will in the world, there are some things on which Christians and Jews will disagree if they remain Christians and Jews. Ultimately, the point of division is that the word of the Lord did not simply come to Jesus of Nazareth, but that in the orthodox Christian point of view, the word of the Lord is Jesus of Nazareth, the word made flesh. The question Dr. Cohen raised, who do people say that I am?, is the great dividing line, the great point of disagreement.

Perhaps it is all to the good that we come near the end of this session realizing the various points on which we can agree and honestly admitting the point on which we do not agree. Realizing why we do agree and disagree is a way forward toward mutual understanding and respect and one of the goals of dialogue. Perhaps John 1:14, "And the Word became flesh and dwelt among us," is the clearest expression of where and why we disagree. Perhaps John knew this very well when he wrote those words that they were the dividing line. With that awareness and respect for difference we have already come a long way toward mutual understanding.

Peter Steinfels: In neither presentation was there use of the word "messiah." Would you each say a word about the place of this concept in the Jewishness of Jesus?

John Meier: When it comes to the question of Messiah, you are getting into my volume 3. What titles, if any titles used of Jesus in the Gospels, actually go back either to himself or to his followers during the public ministry? That is a very tricky question. We have to be aware that not every Jew in first-century Palestine was thinking about, talking about, or expecting the Messiah. Some people were; perhaps a lot of people were not. We can pick up on what Dr. Cohen said about apocalyptic exceptions. If we take a look at the so-called apocalyptic literature, some works are expecting some sort of Messiah, others are quite happy to dispense with a Messiah even within an apocalyptic context.

What is of interest is the fact that Jesus of Nazareth was not only called Messiah at least very early after his death, if not during his lifetime, but was *so* identified with this title that by the time of the writings of Paul, in the first generation of Christianity, Messiah (= Christ) had become practically his second name. All this is especially odd since there was no one fixed expectation of a Messiah or agreement on the meaning of Messiah at the time, and a belief in a Messiah was by no means determinative of Jewish belief and practice. Whence, therefore, this fierce emphasis on the designation of Jesus as Messiah to the point that it becomes practically his second name? I am not sure of the answer here. It may point to the fact that there was something back in the public ministry, either in the teaching and activity of Jesus or at least among his disciples, which led toward this identification. Far from being self-explanatory, I believe messiahship is a great question mark in the study of the historical Jesus and the transition to the early church.

Shaye Cohen: We all know that Jews and Christians argue about Jesus as Messiah. Christians say he was, Jews say he was not. But this is to misstate the argument because Jews and Christians use the word "messiah" to mean different things. What "Messiah" meant in the first century, as Fr. Meier just mentioned, will have varied tremendously from document to document and from group to group. Before Jews and Christians debate whether or not Jesus was the Messiah, they need to ask first what a—or the—Messiah is. What role does the Messiah play in the cosmic order? What is the Messiah supposed to do, and what effect is he supposed to have? On these questions, which logically must precede the question of Jesus' messianic claims, there are fundamental debates between Judaism and Christianity as normatively defined. This point is often lost in the discussion.

Audience member: For two thousand years, the Jews have suffered the consequences of the crucifixion. Why? How can the priesthood educate the people?

John Meier: The question points out that what the earliest Christians saw as shock and scandal, and yet as revelation of God's paradoxical love for sinful humanity, easily became perverted into a weapon by which one religious group beat another over the head. There can be no greater perversion of the cross as a sign of God's redemptive love than precisely such perversion. There is an old Latin axiom: "*Corruptio optimi pessima est*: There is nothing worse than the corruption of the best."

There is the cry in the Gospel, "Away with him, away with him, crucify him." Something very interesting has happened in the restored vernacular liturgies of Palm Sunday and Good Friday as they exist now: the passion Gospels are divided up among three readers in the sanctuary, and the congregation takes the part of the crowd. Hence it is the Christian worshipping "crowd" that now speaks the words "away with him, away with him, crucify him." I remember one lovely lady telling me after the Good Friday liturgy that she was so upset speaking those words. Yes, it was very upsetting. But finally, perhaps we realize the force of the Gospel, that we in this worshipping congregation have spoken those words, not someone else back there. Far from projecting that guilt on anyone else, we take that guilt upon ourselves and say to ourselves, "thou art the person." By a strange inversion, we perhaps finally come back to what the original message was before it was perverted.

The Death of Jesus

November 17, 1994

Burton L. Visotzky: I am very pleased to be here at Fordham. I was in the audience last year when we heard Shaye Cohen and John Meier, with Peter Steinfels as moderator in the first of the *Nostra Aetate* dialogues, when they spoke on the Jewishness of Jesus. Since then it seems I have been caught up in the swirl of the Jewish–Christian dialogue. In the last six months I myself have been traveling the globe for dialogues. In July I was in Warsaw, Poland, where the International Council of Christians and Jews, inevitably due to the locale, confronted the Holocaust. Just a week and a half ago I was in Tulsa, Oklahoma, where we spoke about covenantal dialogue. Today I am delighted to be back in New York City and firmly ensconced in my favorite century—the first. I feel much safer there than dealing with the twentieth century.

Nevertheless, I am fully cognizant of the difficulty of tonight's topic. I want to focus on that difficulty by recalling an episode from my childhood in Chicago. As some of you know, Chicago is the center of a large Catholic population. It is the city with the second largest aggregate of Poles next to Warsaw. And of course there is a large Irish Catholic population.

I grew up in a Jewish neighborhood in Chicago. Just down the block there was a Catholic parochial school called Saint Tim's, and as a kid I used to ride my bike in the schoolyard in St. Tim's. I can still close my eyes and recall being knocked off my bicycle one time by a group of kids from the Catholic school. I knew they were from the school because they were all wearing Saint Timothy uniforms. And as they kicked me and hit me they called me Christ killer. I had no idea what they meant.

I knew enough about Christianity to know there was a Christmas and perhaps Easter. But I did not know enough, at that tender age, to know that Easter might have been related to the death of Christ and, worse, might have involved Jewish complicity in the death of Christ. I was certainly too innocent to know that Jews had suffered my fate and far worse for close to two thousand years.

Tonight I find myself engaged in moderating a dialogue with two great scholars who work precisely on this issue. After they each speak, I will pose a difficult question to each of them. After they have the opportunity to answer these questions, it will be your opportunity to ask questions.

Raymond E. Brown: Part of what makes Holy Week holy is the solemn reading of two Gospel passion narratives, one from the first three Gospels on Passion (Palm) Sunday, and the one from John, every year on Good Friday. It can be fairly claimed that these masterpieces have given more inspiration to artists, musicians, poets, and mystics than any other sections of the New Testament. Ironically, however, such dramatic power makes sensitive Christians uneasy about anti-Jewish elements in the passion narratives. How can they be proclaimed without adding to the tragic history of their misuse against the Jewish people?

Some time ago I brought out a very long commentary on the passion narratives, *The Death of the Messiah* (New York: Doubleday, 1994), the primary focus of which was the positive message that the evangelists wished to convey to their Christian hearers and readers. In it I gave considerable attention to the danger of anti-Judaism in our reactions, but here I want to concentrate on the evolution of anti-Judaism in New Testament thought about the passion to help us to understand how our oldest religious ancestors approached the death of Jesus. I dedicate this essay to the struggle to appreciate the truth and beauty of the narratives without arousing hostility.

There are two approaches I firmly reject. Throughout the centuries and still today the passion narratives have been read as literal history. Such an interpretation produces a view of the Jewish leaders as scheming liars who knowingly deceived the Roman prefect in order to bring about Jesus' death. Matthew's and John's use of the generalizing description of these opponents of Jesus as "Jews" has too often been heard without historical perceptivity as referring to Jews of later centuries and thus has contributed to ongoing hate. This approach has now been firmly rejected in

Roman Catholicism, whether or not all Catholics know this. In 1964 the Roman Pontifical Biblical Commission taught authoritatively that the Gospels are the product of considerable narrative, organizational, and theological development and so are not simply literal accounts of the ministry of Jesus. The next year Vatican Council II explicitly condemned an outlook that would blame the passion without distinction on all the Jews then living or on the Jews today. (See the Council's "Declaration on the Relationship of the Church to Non-Christian Religions" [1965], No. 4).

The other view I judge unacceptable discredits the Gospel passion narratives as almost totally the product of Christian imagination, with little or no foundation in fact. Under the mantle of scholarly objectivity, advocates assert firmly but without proof that the early Christians knew little about how Jesus died and simply invented their narratives on the basis of Old Testament imagery. Indeed, some scholars (of Christian upbringing) would paint them as creating lies precisely to vilify the Jews. If the literalist interpretation of the passion narratives can produce hate toward Judaism, this interpretation can have the effect of portraying Christianity as a false and hateful religion. Religiously sensitive Jews and Christians recognize that if either group of our respective first-century ancestors is presented as liars who wanted to destroy their opposites, nothing has been gained in the ongoing Jewish–Christian dialogue.

A careful examination suggests that the situation in the first century was far more complex than such overly simple reconstructions allow. Let me attempt to do at least partial justice to the complexities by describing four stages in the development of New Testament attitudes toward the death of Jesus.

Stage One: What Happened in A.D. 30 or 33 when Jesus Was Executed on a Cross

Without attempting to repeat all the evidence amassed in *The Death of the Messiah*, a very plausible case can be made for the following. Jesus upset and even alarmed some of his coreligionists by his attitudes toward some legal demands, his assumptions about his own unique teaching authority, his association with sinners, and his critique of public practices that he regarded as meaningless religiosity. Rumors that he might be the Messiah (whether promoted by friends or opponents) caused tension. This came to a head when in Jerusalem he castigated and/or publicly acted out a critique of the Temple procedures and the sanctuary—a sensitive issue economically, socially, and politically. A Sanhedrin or meeting involving the high priest and other important Jerusalem figures decided that he was a dangerous and arrogant (that is to say, blasphemous) nuisance and arranged for him to be seized and handed over to the Roman authorities.

That Jesus could have been manhandled and abused in such an arrest and transferal would be far from surprising. For the Roman governor he was not a major threat. (Pilate's prefecture up to this time saw occasional protests and riots, but not the armed revolutionary movements of an earlier or later period, when the Romans sent out troops and executed hundreds without any pretense at trial.) Nevertheless, Jesus was potentially a menace if people thought he was a messiah or king, and so Pilate ordered Jesus executed.

The historical plausibility of this Gospel picture can be supported from Josephus, the Jewish historian who wrote his *Antiquities* at the end of the first century A.D. Amid his account of Pilate's governorship (including several instances of crowds assembling to put pressure on him), Josephus refers to Pilate's treatment of Jesus. Serious scholarship would now judge the following to have been authentic in that reference: Jesus was a wise man who did astonishing deeds and taught many people, but "Pilate condemned him to the cross in indictment of the first-ranking men among us."

From Josephus's description of what happened thirty years later to another man called Jesus (the son of Ananias), we learn how such an indictment might have worked. This other Jesus cried out a message against Jerusalem and the Temple sanctuary. By such behavior he provoked the leading citizens, who, thinking he was under some supernatural drive, had him beaten and led him before the Roman governor. The latter had him scourged, but he would not respond. (He was finally let go as a maniac but was killed in the siege of Jerusalem.) A combination of the Josephus accounts show how exaggerated are the claims that the substance of the Gospel portrayals of the treatment of Jesus of Nazareth cannot be historical.

STAGE TWO:
CHRISTIANS INTERPRETED THE PASSION OF JESUS AGAINST A SCRIPTURAL BACKGROUND

Neither the claim of wholesale invention nor the failure to recognize a creative rethinking does justice to what happened next. The New Testament is insistent that what befell Jesus matched what was found in the Law and the prophets. In particular, the Old Testament portraits of how the just suffered at the hands of the wicked colored memories preserved by Jesus' followers.

Historically, the motives of the authorities aligned against Jesus at the time of his execution were surely a mixture: genuine religious outrage at his actions and claims, worry about civic unrest, crass self-interest, fear of his provoking Roman intervention, and so on. But now a quest for what was theologically significant motivated simplification; those opposed to Jesus took on the biblical coloring of the wicked who plot against the innocent. For instance, in Wisdom 2:17–21 the wicked contend that if the just one be the son of God, God will defend him; and they resolve to revile him and put him to death. The abuse and travail of Jesus takes on the plaintive tones of the hymnist of Psalm 22 and the Suffering Servant of Isaiah 52–53. For his followers, Jesus' sufferings cast light on such passages, which illumined the role of Jesus' death in the plan of God.

This stage of reflection on the passion was not anti-Jewish, any more than were the psalms or other biblical books that were mined for this imagery. After all, the just one, his admirers, and the wicked opponents were all Jews. And the theological simplification of the opponents as wicked is a standard biblical portrayal, not a nefarious Christian falsification. Six hundred years before, not all who disagreed with Jeremiah's policies for Judah were wicked; but the biblical accounts portrays them thus, simplifying their motives and dramatizing their actions. Indeed, some of the most sensitive words in the passion of Jesus are found in Jeremiah

26. When, with God's authority, Jeremiah threatened the destruction of the Temple, the priests and *all the people* heard him, and the priests and the prophets demanded his death. Jeremiah warned them that they were bringing *innocent* blood in Jerusalem and its citizens.

STAGE THREE:
THE BEGINNING OF THE USE OF "JEWS" TO DESCRIBE ONE OF THE
TWO GROUPS ARRAYED AGAINST JESUS

As we can tell from Paul's writings, a major factor in this stage was the conversion of Gentiles to the following of Jesus. The Apostle encountered hostility from synagogue authorities in his proclamation of the Gospel, as he indicates in 2 Corinthians 11:24: ("From the Jews on five occasions I received the 39 lashes"), and so did his Gentile converts, according to Acts. Paul compared the enmity Christians were experiencing to that endured by Jesus, employing in 1 Thessalonians 2:14–15 (a passage that I firmly contend is genuine) a description of *"the Jews who killed the Lord Jesus* and the prophets and who persecuted us.*"* In itself that could be simply a distinguishing classification (the Jews, as distinct from the Romans, who had a role in Jesus' death); but the further assimilation to hostile Jewish authorities encountered both by Paul and his readers tells us that two decades after Jesus' death his passion was entering into debates between Jews who did not accept Jesus and Jews and Gentiles who did.

How much anti-Judaism was involved in this use of "Jews" for the Jerusalem authorities who had a role in Jesus' death? A number of factors governed the issue. For instance, how hostile was the experience of the readers or hearers with Jews who rejected the proclamation of Jesus? At this early period Christian Jews who used such language may at other times have been nostalgic about their Jewish heritage (as Paul was in Romans 9:3–5). The same would not have been true of Gentile Christians; indeed, they may have read into an expression like "the Jews who killed the Lord Jesus" prejudices against Jews stemming from their own Gentile background. Was equal hostility showed by Christians toward the Romans who had a role in the death of Jesus? It probably depended on whether Roman authority had harried the Christians. The psalm application in Acts 4:25–27 places in equal array against Jesus "Herod and Pontius Pilate, the Gentiles and the people of Israel." In Gospel portrayals the mockery of Jesus by Roman soldiers is more brutal than that by Jewish authorities or police.

STAGE FOUR:
THE USE OF "JEWS" TO DESCRIBE THOSE INVOLVED IN THE DEATH
OF JESUS IN CIRCUMSTANCES WHEN THE CHRISTIANS WERE NO
LONGER "JEWS"

Paul's phrase, "the Jews who killed Jesus," was restrictive to one group of Jews; but before long such language would have been generalized, particularly as at different places at different moments the majority among the Christians who used it was not ethnically Jewish. More delicately, because of alienation (and at times of expulsion) from synagogues, some ethnically Jewish Christians were no longer using the term "Jews" of themselves. That seems to be the case among some of the Christians reflected in the Gospels of John and Matthew. Accordingly, when a major role in the passion of Jesus was attributed to "the Jews," the impression was now being given that another people (different from us Christians) was involved. When Matthew 27:25 was read ("All the people said, 'His blood on us and on our children'"), that other people was taking on the responsibility for the death of Jesus. Indeed, the reference to "children" here in Luke 23:38 ("Daughters of Jerusalem . . . for yourselves weep and for your children") suggests that the Roman defeat of the Jews and the destruction of the Jerusalem Temple in A.D. 70 were perceived as God's punishment for having put Jesus to death. It is not surprising that Christians would make such a judgment, given that Josephus (*Antiquities* 20.8.5) gave an analogous theological explanation: God turned away from Jerusalem and allowed the Romans to burn the city because of hate for the impiety, murders, and profanation among Jews there in the fifties and sixties.

Some of the alleviating factors in Stage Three were now gone, and the parallel between "the Jews" who were hostile to Jesus and contemporary Jews who did not accept Jesus and were looked on as hostile to Christians became complete. (And one may guess that on the other side, among some Jews, a parallel was drawn between "that fellow" who caused trouble forty or fifty years ago and the present troublemakers who were making blasphemous claims about him.) One catches elements of that connection in a passage like Matthew 28:12–15, where a lie that the disciples stole the body of Jesus, started through a bribe given by the chief priests and elders, "has been spread among Jews until this day." If at this stage we can finally speak of anti-Judaism, notice that it had taken time to develop, was not intrinsic to the passion itself, and reflects the unfriendly relationship between Christians (ethnically Jew or Gentile) and Jews who did not believe in Jesus.

Stage Four was only the beginning of a long history; by the next century Christians would be accusing Jews of deicide (Melito of Sardis), and Jewish legends (reflected in the pagan Celsus' attacks on Christianity) were portraying Jesus as a wicked magician and the illegitimate son of an adulteress. The effect of the hostile feelings became one-sided after the conversion of Constantine to Christianity and the gaining of political power by Christians. This was the beginning of a tragic history that would see the oppression and persecution of Jews continue through the centuries, culminating horrendously in our own. Many non-Christian elements contributed to that history, particularly in the Nazi period; but often the passion narratives were read in a way that fueled hatred of Jews.

In efforts to ensure that this never happen again, what I have contended above may serve well. The recognition that important Jewish figures in Jerusalem were hostile to Jesus and had a role in his death need not of itself have produced anti-Judaism, any more than the fact that the Jerusalem priests and prophets plotted Jeremiah's death would produce such a result. The first Christian attempt to see the theological significance in Jesus' death by use of the scriptural portrayal of the just persecuted by the wicked did not of itself have an anti-Jewish tone. Anti-Judaism appeared when the death was interpreted through the optic of the then-existing bad relations between believers in Jesus (often no longer ethnically Jewish) and Jews who did not believe in him.

Good relations between Christians and Jews, based on respect for each other, are the optic that will most facilitate the reading of the passion narratives without an anti-Jewish effect. Christians who appreciate the great heritage of Judaism will work sensitively to correct the simplification whereby those hostile to Jesus are portrayed without qualification as "the Jews."

We Christians cannot dismiss or deny what happened to Jesus—that is too facile an escapism. In liturgically celebrating the truth and power of the passion narratives, however, we must be equally energetic in proclaiming, as did Pope John Paul II on the Auschwitz anniversary: "Never again anti-Semitism."

Michael J. Cook: About 650 years ago, a colossal sculpture of Jesus upon the cross, with Mary and St. John at his feet, was being carted up a steep incline toward its present site: a towering eminence overlooking Oberammergau, a hamlet in Bavaria. As that statue was being attended to by its sculptor, the wagon carrying it suddenly slipped. The statue, toppling toward the ground, fell upon its sculptor, its creator, and crushed him to death!

Such a macabre tragedy might, ordinarily, prompt us to wonder about that sculptor—his family, his talents, his ambitions. An additional reaction, however, was forthcoming from Joseph Krauskopf, a rabbi touring Oberammergau at the turn of the century. He preferred to bypass the victim as a person in favor of the victim as a *symbol*: That sculptor's fate conjured up the oppression of the Jewish people by their own creation, Christianity! Did not Judaism sculpt Christianity—raising up its founders, Jesus and Paul, and supplying the new religion's potential for assuming colossal dimension? In turn, as Christianity began its ascent toward its own towering eminence, did it not topple, as it were, upon the Jews, its creative source, as if to quash them? In this instance, the sculptor—the Jewish people—at least managed to survive, but only by continuously bearing up under onerous prejudicial stereotypes.[1]

Krauskopf's imagery conveys how impelled modern Jews feel to move, in some measure, beyond what happened to Jesus alone back in the early first century, and to discuss his death also in

---

[1] Joseph A. Krauskopf, *A Rabbi's Impressions of the Oberammergau Passion Play* (Philadelphia: Edward Stern, 1901), p. 20.

terms of its wider ramifications for the Jewish people ever after. Even Christian theologians—mindful of how injurious have been the consequences of Jesus' death for Jews throughout history— have sometimes cited Jesus, the Jew upon the cross, as a metaphor for the crucifixion of the *Jews*! Meanwhile, many historians, Jewish and non-Jewish alike, have abetted this trend, contending that the Gospel passion portraits of Jesus' trial and execution reflect the overlay of anti-Jewish animosity from the Evangelists' own later day. This determination has led some to process the passion narratives in a fashion that minimizes, if not eliminates altogether, any notion of Jewish complicity in Jesus' arrest and execution.

However much Jews may appreciate this addressing—indeed, redressing—of grievances over texts from the distant past, the question arises: is it truly plausible to insist on little, even *no*, Jewish involvement in Jesus' death?[2] Raymond Brown strongly dissents in his monumental study, *The Death of the Messiah*, whose recent publication is the primary impetus for tonight's program. Accordingly, it behooves me both to outline how Jews are likely to react to his views as well as to advance my personal assessment of his stance.

AFFIRMING JEWISH "RESPONSIBILITY" IN JESUS' DEATH: THE STANCE OF RAYMOND BROWN

Relatively few Jews will welcome Fr. Brown's analysis specifically of Jesus' arrest and trial. For the essential thrust of his findings has been to reaffirm much of the *underlying* accuracy of the very Gospel accounts which Jews have now become accustomed to contesting, and to call into question some mainstays of what has emerged as the conventional Jewish position on Jesus' death. Jews will commonly recite a string of rabbinic capital trial procedures, many of them protective of the defendant, to "prove" that Jesus could not have been tried by Jews in the fashion in which the Gospels allege. But Fr. Brown relegates the rabbinic presentation of such procedures to a later, and non-relevant, time-frame (pp.

---

[2] See especially P. L. Maier, "Who Killed Jesus?" *Christianity Today* 34 (1990), pp. 16–19.

357–63). Moreover, he challenges the assumption that *Roman* officialdom had to have been the driving force behind Jesus' arrest and that Jesus was merely one more casualty among countless others at the hands of a *ruthless* Pontius Pilate. The oppressiveness of Roman rulers as early as Jesus' day has been overdrawn, he feels, as also the presumption of a countryside then teeming with messianic pretenders and subversives. Fr. Brown insists that only as we approach the Jewish Revolt of 66 C.E. do we see a proliferation of Jewish seditious activity *now* matched by a corresponding intensification of Roman watchfulness and brutality (pp. 21ff.; 677ff.); we must therefore be careful not to presuppose that conditions and policies characterizing the *second* set of Roman prefects (44–66 C.E.) likewise typified those of Pontius Pilate and fellow governors of the first set (6–41 C.E.).

Instead, it strikes Fr. Brown as far more plausible that Jesus was indeed arrested by *Jewish* leaders who gave him over to Pilate, in fundamental consistency with the rudimentary Gospel portrait— and also with the testimony of the genuine[3] Josephus and rabbinic writings[4] (both accepting that, as a matter of course, Jesus was arrested by Jewish leaders). Actions taken against other perceived troublemakers roughly contemporaneous with Jesus likewise featured prominent involvement by Jewish authorities. Especially telling is the circumstance that the Jerusalem church's ongoing problems *continued* to be with the Jewish priestly circle rather than with Rome—i.e., with the same elements as those which the Gospels themselves insist had orchestrated Jesus' capture and condemnation (pp. 363–72; 540ff.).

In sum, therefore, Fr. Brown traces the impetus to arrest Jesus not to Rome after all, but rather to Jewish leaders who came to pronounce Jesus a blasphemer (on any one of a variety of possible

---

[3] Josephus' description of Jesus (*Antiquities* 18:63–64) includes the statement that Jesus was put to death "upon the indictment of the first-ranking men among us." Acknowledging that other elements of this paragraph betray tampering by a later hand, Fr. Brown nonetheless retains *this* clause as genuinely Josephan (pp. 373ff.). Cf. also John P. Meier, *A Marginal Jew: Rethinking the Historical Jesus* (New York: Doubleday, 1991), pp. 59ff.

[4] That the rabbis may here only be depending upon the Gospels' own story-line is a consideration which, in my view, Fr. Brown understates. Cf., however, p. 17*n*23.

bases[5]) precisely as the Gospel Sanhedrin scenes report (pp. 532, 544ff.). While developments of the Gospel writers' own later day assuredly influenced the way the Evangelists depicted events back during Jesus' lifetime, Fr. Brown defends the basic accuracy of the traditions underlying a Sanhedrin deliberation,[6] Jesus' condemnation for blasphemy, and his hearing before Pilate.[7]

At the same time, Fr. Brown insists on distinguishing "responsibility" from "blame." He is open to the possibilities that Jesus was a person capable of generating intense dislike and that reasonable, even righteous, Jewish officials (genuinely offended by Jesus) may have felt sincere in believing his execution warranted. But while such religiosity may mitigate a sense of their *blame*, it would not diminish their *responsibility* (pp. 383ff.; 391ff.).[8]

AN ALTERNATIVE STANCE

It is incumbent upon modern Jews looking askance at Fr. Brown's findings to examine his detailed argumentation before passing judgment. The formidable erudition he displays in all other aspects of his work is not likely suspended when he attempts to isolate those responsible in Jesus' death.

At the same time, I incline to the view that circumstances of the Gospel writers' own day determined some of the *basics* of what they wrote concerning the Jews' role in Jesus' death. Accordingly, I question Fr. Brown's contention that Jesus was genuinely charged with *blasphemy*; instead, I believe this tradition

---

[5] E.g., that Jesus said he spoke for God, put himself in place of God, claimed to be Christ (Messiah) and Son of God, spoke and acted against the Temple, etc.

[6] Albeit that it "took place some time before Jesus was arrested" (p. 586).

[7] "I reject [the] thesis that would drive a wedge between the PNs [Passion Narratives] as accounts of the trial of Jesus and the PNs as accounts of Christian reactions to Jews and Romans at the time of Gospel writing. The second stage has influenced the portrayal of the first, but one must respect the important influence of preGospel evidence about what happened to Jesus" (p. 387n138).

[8] Disconcertingly, however, the *Nostra Aetate* statement (which Brown defends [p. 385]) is usually rendered only in terms of "blame": Jesus' death "cannot be *blamed* upon all the Jews then living" (emphasis mine; reference here is to Section 4 of the fuller Ecumenical Council Vatican II document [October 28, 1965] titled "Declaration on the Relationship of the Church to Non-Christian Religions").

originated from later Jewish assessments of *contemporary* Christians as blasphemers. I have additional reservations about the actuality of a presumed Sanhedrin interrogation focusing on Jesus and even about the historicity of Jesus' hearing before Pilate. I am disposed to chalk up more of the Evangelists' testimony to their free improvisation (rather than to their reliance upon sources or tradition), and I also believe that they drew upon Jewish Scriptural motifs to *generate* certain aspects of Jesus' life-story not rooted in fact.

Nonetheless, I do grant the essential plausibility of Fr. Brown's case that *some* Jewish involvement was integral in the events leading to Jesus' execution. I also applaud his efforts to differentiate responsibility from blame. Yet once he broaches this distinction, does he extend his argument far enough? For does not some "responsibility" in Jesus' death adhere also to *Jesus personally*? And what of "responsibility" for the later deaths of countless *additional* Jews attributable to the way Gospel texts were enlisted as pretexts for pogroms and other persecutions? I know that many Christians will find the following notion extremely disconcerting: In the Jewish view, given the preciousness which Judaism accords to *every* human life,[9] undeserved deaths of *other* righteous persons— including those of other righteous Jews—may be no less tragic than that of Jesus personally. The question of responsibility might therefore well apply to all such deaths *equally.*

It will be helpful to compartmentalize these matters into three consecutive time frames: (A) that of Jesus' ministry; (B) that of the Gospel writers; and (C) that of later history.

A. Jesus' Ministry

I configure Jesus' mission as follows:[10]

1. Jesus saw himself as God's last envoy before God's imminent direct intervention in history, not by any force of human arms

---

[9] Intriguingly, this is most emphasized in Mishnah *Sanhedrin* (4:5) itself, in conjunction with capital trial procedures!

[10] My own conclusions dovetail with those of E. P. Sanders, upon whom I draw extensively; see his *Jesus and Judaism* (Philadelphia: Fortress, 1985); idem, *The Historical Figure of Jesus* (London: Penguin, 1993).

but rather by a mighty, Divine act. This intervention would result in the elimination of evil and evildoers; in the building of a new and more glorious temple; and in the reassembly of the people of Israel. Outcasts—such as the poor, meek, and lowly (even the wicked)—would now achieve places of acceptance.

2. Also in this coming "kingdom" of God, Jesus' disciples would play some important role,[11] subsidiary to an even more prominent, possibly *kingly*, role for their leader.

3. Jesus heralded this new kingdom's arrival, and his own role in it, through symbolic demonstrations,[12] primarily an entry into Jerusalem under the guise of a humble king riding upon an ass; an overturning of tables of moneychangers in the temple; and a celebration of his Last Supper as an anticipation of a messianic banquet.

4. Of these demonstrations, his action in the temple was the most critical.[13] His overturning of temple furniture was intended to symbolize the change of eras—the overturning of the current world order in favor of its replacement by the coming new kingdom (the ruling power of God).

5. His announcement of the coming kingdom stirred the hopes of some listeners but also the concerns of others. Since presum-

---

[11] "You yourselves will be seated upon twelve thrones judging the twelve tribes of Israel" (Matthew 19:28); also the request by James and John to sit at either side of Jesus in the kingdom (Mark 10:37 & parallels)—traditions whose authenticity Sanders defends in *Jesus and Judaism*, pp. 98–106; 233ff.; 237; cf. *Figure*, pp. 120ff.

[12] Prophets' singular (even weird) performances, charged with dire meaning, were deemed instrumental in bringing God's will to pass: Ahijah (1 Kings 11:29ff.) rips a garment into twelve pieces and gives ten to Jeroboam (= the wresting of ten Northern tribes from the South); Jeremiah (13:6ff.) purchases a linen waistcloth (its spoilage = the way Jehoiakim's pro-Babylonian foreign policy *spoiled* the pride of Judah and Jerusalem); (in 32:1ff.) he purchases land in Anathoth (dramatizing his confidence in Judah's future); Ezekiel (in 4:1ff.) takes a sun-dried brick and draws in relief Jerusalem under siege, and uses an iron plate, a griddle, to symbolize God's role in Jerusalem's fall; (in 4:4–6) he lies 390 days on his left side (to symbolize the years of Israel's punishment) and forty days on his right side (to symbolize that of Judah); he takes a sharp sword (5:1ff.) and cuts off hair and beard (shorn hair symbolizing the fate in store for the people); he dramatizes by appropriate actions (12:1ff.) the gathering of whatever belongings the exiles could carry; (in 37:15ff.) he joins two sticks together (symbolizing the re-establishment of a united Israel).

[13] "Before 70 AD disputes over the Temple constituted the most frequent single factor in religious violence among Jews" (Brown, *Death*, p. 18).

ably the personnel ruling a new kingdom would be *different* from that now governing the old, those most acutely provoked would have been the then current leaders, the chief priestly elements. Jesus' demonstration in the temple was decisive in prompting priestly intercession against him.

6. Although the followers Jesus attracted were sufficiently noticeable for Jesus himself to be construed a danger, his inner circle seemed innocuous enough to obviate need for *their* capture as well.

7. That Jesus was being hailed by at least some followers as a "king," and may have thought this of himself, constituted information conveyed by the high priest Caiaphas to Pontius Pilate, who then consigned this irritating Galilean to the cross.

8. Jesus' parables of the coming kingdom, his intimation that he would play a role (perhaps a royal one) in that kingdom, and his entry into Jerusalem as a humble king may have all contributed to the Roman accusation (atop the cross) that Jesus had thought of himself as would-be "*king* of the Jews."

B. The Age of the Gospel Writers

While such may be the essential contours of Jesus' ministry itself (ca. 30 C.E.), I am even more concerned with the time-frame of the Gospel writers roughly forty to seventy years later. It is their depictions of Jesus which have so adversely affected the Jewish people over the centuries. In their own day, the four Evangelists were ill-disposed toward Jews who would not accept Jesus. This animosity likely impacted the way the Gospels came to present traditions of Jewish involvement in Jesus' death: intensifying and aggrandizing any role played by Jews, impugning their motives, maligning their character. Accordingly, the theoretical question arises: *which* dynamic was the more *potent* in bringing us to our current Gospel portraits—that some Jewish officials may have actually become instrumental in Jesus' arrest and condemnation, or that ill-will toward Jews-rejecting-Jesus in the Gospel writers' own later day may have determined, even *necessitated,* the Evangelists' presentation of the Jews as chief culprits?

Major considerations from the political, social, and religious contexts of the Gospel writers demand our attention:

Wariness of Rome

By the last third of the first century, as the Gospels were achieving completion, Christian communities had reason to feel apprehensive of Rome. The Emperor Nero is said to have scapegoated Christians, in 64 C.E., for a fire in Rome (Tacitus, *Annals* xv, 44), and to have inflicted upon them "grievous torments" (Suetonius, *Life of Nero* 16). Is this information substantially correct? If so, does at least the earliest Gospel, Mark (ca. 70)—whether or not written in Rome[14]—reflect wariness of this localized occurrence? Also, were Christians generally, including those outside Rome, cognizant of—and, if so, distressed by—this anti-Christian offensive by Roman officialdom?

In 66, moreover, Jews of the Holy Land launched a major revolt against Rome. Rome's brutal vengeance could well have signaled danger also to any followers of Christianity likely to be identified with rebellious Jews. Such confusion was possible since many Christians appeared to share not only Jewish Scripture but also facets of Jewish belief and practice—in some cases, even Jewish family ties. Since, as Fr. Brown likewise insists, "hostile anti-Christian propaganda of the post-70 period surely equated Jesus with the Jews who made trouble for the Roman order" (p. 688), the Gospel writers may well have deemed it advisable to dissociate the Jesus movement in their own day from the sullied image of seditious Jews.

The Jewish revolt, we should understand, had badly shaken the Roman people.[15] Starting with the ignominious defeat of a Roman army, the war embarrassingly dragged on four years and also portended danger from the Parthians, Rome's inveterate enemy, who seemed poised to invade Rome's eastern provinces (in ostensible support of the Jewish insurgents). Such considerations catalyzed the eventual staging in Rome itself of a special

---

[14] See my argument in *Mark's Treatment of the Jewish Leaders* (Leiden: Brill, 1978), pp. 10ff.; cf. Brown, p. 9n8.

[15] I follow here especially S. G. F. Brandon, *The Trial of Jesus of Nazareth* (New York: Stein & Day, 1968), pp. 68ff.

pageantry celebrating Rome's triumph over Judea. Among the spoils prominently exhibited were treasures brought from Jerusalem's Temple: the glorious seven-branched lampstand (*menorah*), the golden table of shewbread, and the purple curtains that veiled the sanctuary. (Later, images of such accoutrements became enshrined on sculptured panels of the Arch of Titus, in the Roman Forum.)

Among those witnessing this spectacle could well have been Christians disconcerted that treasures of the Temple—now displayed as tokens of its destruction and Israel's overthrow—symbolized a cult with which their own faith was indissolubly linked. How discomfited they would have been by the perception that the founder to whom they traced their movement was known himself to have undergone crucifixion, a *Roman* punishment (often for *subversives*), and that the movement tracing itself to him stemmed from Palestine, a land now indelibly tied, in the Roman mind, to fanatical rebellion! Whatever, therefore, the reality of who had actually brought Jesus to execution back around the year 30, the question at a *later* date could have remained: To what degree would a *crucified* Jesus have invited speculation by outsiders not only that Christianity's founder and Lord had been himself a seditionist but that this same stigma should now adhere likewise to Jesus' *later followers*?[16]

Thus would the Evangelists have incorporated many traditions (including ones authentic to Jesus' ministry) with an eye to distancing the Jesus who had died on the cross decades earlier from any hint of sedition. They would also have been disposed to present, on behalf of later Christian communities, an impression of Christianity's benign nature and orientation vis-à-vis Rome—not as much an affirmation of *loyalty* to Rome as a determination that *neither Jesus himself nor his later followers should be thought guilty of any crime against Rome or deemed in any respect deserving of Roman imprisonment, let alone death.*[17] Typical of traditions so included

---

[16] A related question troubling to Christians was "how . . . could Gentiles seriously . . . regard a convicted insurrectionist as a God-man able to redeem them?" (W. R. Wilson, *The Execution of Jesus* [New York: Scribner's, 1970], p. 79).

[17] Brown, *Death*, p. 390n144.

would have been Jesus' dictum to "render to Caesar the things that are Caesar's" (Mark 12:17 & parallels), as well as many Gospel suggestions that Jesus was a pacifist: e.g., his stated insistence that "all who take the sword will perish by the sword" (Matthew 26:52) and his query in Gethsemane, "have you come out as against a robber [= seditionist?], with swords and clubs to capture me?" (Mark 14:48 & parallels); also, pronouncement of Jesus' innocence by a subversive[18] flanking him on the cross (Luke 23:41)[19] in addition to presentation of Barabbas the insurrectionist as the foil for a non-subversive Jesus of Nazareth (Mark 15:7ff. & parallels). Also consistent with this pattern would be Gospel *attenuations*[20] of Jesus' symbolic gesture in the temple,[21] of his prediction of the temple's fall (Mark 13:1 & parallels)[22] and of his

---

[18] Brown himself argues (p. 688) that the co-crucified "thieves" (*lestai*; singular: *lestes*) are better understood in the writings of *the Evangelists'* day as seditionists: "the evangelists and their audiences . . . may have associated Barabbas and those crucified beside Jesus . . . with the revolutionaries of the . . . Jewish Revolt of AD 66–70, types from whom they carefully distinguished Jesus"—a consideration which should inform our understanding of *lestes* in the preceding example, now to be read: "Have you come out [against me] as against a *seditionist* . . . ?"

[19] Should we accept the historicity of those flanking Jesus, or were these generated by the "Suffering Servant" motif in Isaiah 53:12 ("because he poured out his soul to death, and was *numbered with the transgressors*")?

[20] All three Synoptists (Mark 11:17; Matthew 21:13; Luke 19:46) have Jesus decry the sanctuary's transformation into a "den of robbers" (conflating Jeremiah 7:11 with Isaiah 56:7), thereby making it appear that Jesus was merely (and reasonably) protesting dishonesty. In this way, they attenuate what might otherwise have appeared an act of *violence* (an impression to be avoided, given Christians' fear of Rome). Jesus' action is then rendered all the more innocuous by depicting his *unimpeded* return to the Temple the very next day (Mark 11:20, 27; Matthew 21:18, 23)!

[21] "Cleansing" was hardly the *intent* of Jesus' Temple action but rather the Evangelists' *camouflage* of that action. Money-changers performed legitimate Temple services necessary if commandments given by God through Moses were to be obeyed (changing pilgrims' currency into coinage acceptable by the Temple, selling certifiedly unblemished animals for sacrifice, etc. (Sanders, *Jesus and Judaism*, pp. 63ff.; idem, *Judaism: Practice and Belief 63 BCE-66 CE* [Philadelphia: Trinity, 1992], pp. 89ff.).

[22] Sanders (*Figure*, p. 257) argues that the temple-prediction ascribed to Jesus must be genuine (not created after the fact) since it was not fulfilled in *all* particulars (the actual destruction was by *fire*, not dismantling or demolition [as per Mark 13:2: "There will not be left here one stone upon another, that will not be thrown down"]).

reputed threat[23] to destroy the temple (Mark 14:57ff.; Matthew 26:60ff.).

Such considerations prompt as well a re-evaluation of Jesus' presumed hearing before the Roman prefect, Pontius Pilate. On some level, the Evangelists intended their portrayal of Pilate's exoneration of Jesus to serve a *symbolic* function: demonstrating that a significant Roman official in Jesus' own day had acquitted him of sedition would dispose later pagans to view Christians of their own day as likewise innocent of subversive activity!

Rancor Toward (Non-Christian) Jews

How could it eventuate that Jesus, if innocent of sedition, had died atop a Roman cross? To recast his execution by Rome in a now distinctly less disturbing light, would not the Gospel writers have been inexorably drawn to present, if at all possible, some other party (i.e., in *addition* to Rome) as also instrumental in Jesus' death? Certainly, a prime candidate lay readily at hand in the Evangelists' *contemporary* opponents, namely, Jews who, rejecting Jesus, were now engaging the Christian community with acrimony. A natural presumption would have been: such belligerence simply *continued* hostility likewise exchanged by the *forebears* of these Jews with Jesus personally! Certainly, by casting Jesus' leading enemies as having been in particular the *chief priests*, the Evangelists could also impress upon pagans that the functionaries operating the Jerusalem *Temple* (which Rome had just burnt) were *successors* of the primary instigators of Jesus' capture and execution! (This would, of course, also suggest, in turn, that the Temple had *deserved* destruction!)

The accounts of Jesus' appearance before Pilate are so congruent with later Christian interests that they must raise doubts as to whether this episode genuinely occurred. Whenever it was,

---

[23] The way the Evangelists treat the threat suggests its genuineness. Mark (14:56ff.) and Matthew (26:59ff.) have it attested to only by *false* witnesses (Luke moves the charge to Acts 6:14 in conjunction with the trial of Stephen). It reappears at the crucifixion: both Mark 15:29 and Matthew 27:40 depict the crowd as calling Jesus "the one who would destroy the temple and rebuild it in three days." Rather than dropping the threat, John (2:19–22) reinterprets it when, following the Temple cleansing, he casts Jesus as speaking of the destroying and raising "of the temple *of his body*"!

however, that the story-line came to cast Pilate as having acquitted Jesus who was then crucified *anyway*, it would have become desirable, even necessary, for Christian writers to propose some other (and necessarily *earlier*) interrogation condemnatory of Jesus and conducted by some party *other* than Pilate! Since contemporary Christians were feeling harassed and rejected by Jewish critics (perhaps even informed-upon, by them, to Rome [cf. Mark 13:12 and parallels]), the Evangelists would likely have supposed that the rancor their fellow-Christians were experiencing in *their* relations with Jewish opponents only *paralleled* that experienced by Jesus personally decades earlier—i.e., that Jesus, too, must have been subjected to similar persecution and prosecution at Jewish hands!

Thus, even as we grant the likelihood that *some* Jewish elements in Jesus' day had indeed been involved in arresting and interrogating Jesus and then in delivering him to Rome, we should not lose sight of the dynamics and motivations operative in the Evangelists' own later age—which not only tended toward *envisioning* the contours of just such a scenario but would now inevitably have done so also in a distortive, if not vindictive, kind of way. Against the backdrop of the great Jewish Revolt and of Christians' wariness of Rome in general, this complex of Gospel traditions would have had the effect of allying Christians with Rome even while presenting "the Jews" as the enemies of both. In this fashion, a *Jew* actually put to death by *Romans* would paradoxically become a *Christian* put to death by *Jews*!

Accordingly, we have two propositions operating here: one, of *actual* responsibility by Jewish authorities; and a second, of the Gospel writers' disposition toward *assigning* responsibility to "the Jews." The two theses so reinforce one another as to suggest the irony that, even if Jews had actually played only a minimal (indeed *no*) role in Jesus' arrest and condemnation, the Evangelists may have been drawn not only to advance but also to *aggrandize* such a role for Jews anyway! The earlier question, then, here bears repetition: which dynamic would likely have become the more *potent* in bringing us to our current Gospel portraits—that there were Jewish officials who actually occasioned Jesus' arrest and condemnation, or that fears and animosities in the Gospel writers'

own later day *determined* the Evangelists' presentation of the Jews
as having been chief culprits?

The Germaneness of "Blasphemy"

Mark (14:53–72) and Matthew (26:57–75) present Jesus as subjected to a formal, elaborate, Sanhedrin trial culminating in his
condemnation for *blasphemy*.[24] Here, too, a need of the Evangelists
themselves could well have been primary in determining the Gospel portrait. Their contemporary Jewish opponents undoubtedly
cast Christians as "blasphemers" for exalting Jesus as divine.
Against such a backdrop, how natural it would have been to presume "blasphemy" as likewise the charge of which Jesus personally had been accused by *his* Jewish contemporaries decades
earlier! Moreover, designating the charge as "blasphemy"—a *religious* offense of concern to Jews only—would have served the
Christian interest by defusing, even eclipsing, suspicion that Jesus
had entertained *political* ambitions (e.g., pretensions to royalty),
this despite the likelihood that "Jesus was delivered to Pilate . . .
because *the fundamental charges against Jesus were never religious in
nature.*"[25]

It is true, of course, that rabbinic literature also came to pronounce Jesus a blasphemer. But the rabbis, writing centuries after
Jesus' death, would here have been drawing not upon any independent recall but rather upon the already long-circulated story-
line advanced by the Gospels themselves! Naturally, the rabbis
would have similarly processed Christian theologies of their *own*
day as blasphemy, and this would have served only to reinforce
the Gospels' own successful *camouflage* of the charge of sedition
(the accusation most likely actually lodged against Jesus).

Christian Reliance Upon Jewish Scripture

The purported grandiosity of Jesus' "Sanhedrin trial" (Mark
14:53, 55ff.; Matthew 26:57, 59ff.) must also raise our suspicions.

---

[24] Luke's less formal hearing omits a charge of blasphemy (though cf. 5:21;
also Acts 6:11). John has a Sanhedrin session (without Jesus) much earlier
(11:47–53), with blasphemy mentioned earlier still (10:33: "The Jews answered
[Jesus], '. . . we stone you for blasphemy; because you, being a man, make
yourself God' ").

[25] Wilson, *Execution*, p. 16.

Any Jewish hearing as originally conceived would, more plausibly, have been but modest in scope—perhaps a simple interrogation which only Jesus' later stature in the Christian mind would have amplified into a full-fledged "courtroom" proceeding.[26] Nor would even this necessarily have been sufficient: for the Evangelists to portray Jesus as having appeared before Jewish officials (let alone the Sanhedrin itself), yet then to confess to knowing few if any specifics as to what had transpired at that appearance, would have seemed artless in a milieu where recording "history" was more art than science. Eventually, there would have ensued a thirst by Christians for ever more details: *where* the court had met; *who* had participated; the precise *charge* lodged against Jesus; *what* he had been asked; *how* he had responded; etc. In this fashion would the original kernel have become expanded and embellished.

Here Christian tradition could well have gathered "information" about Jesus—where real evidence was lacking—by recourse to the Jewish Bible for clues presumably predictive of the Messiah. This would account for Jesus' curious demeanor under fire, where he is depicted as *both* utterly silent and yet stridently outspoken! The incongruity would be due to enlistment of *contrasting* Jewish Biblical motifs: Jesus' "silence" drawn from Isaiah's Suffering Servant who "was oppressed . . . , yet he *opened not his mouth*; like a . . . sheep that before its shearers is *dumb*" (Isaiah 53:7; cf. also Psalm 38:13–16), alongside Jesus' abrupt proclamation that "you will see the Son of man seated at the right hand of Power, and coming with the clouds of heaven" (Mark 14:62), derived from a Danielic vision (7:13[27]) supplemented by Psalm 110:1.[28]

The end result: once we grant that *details* of what transpired in the Sanhedrin scene might well have been drawn from Jewish Scripture, then we are left uncertain as to precisely what actually did occur at Jesus' purported Sanhedrin appearance. As matters

[26] "Only a small handful of temple officials . . . remove[d] Jesus. . . . Later Christian tradition . . . involved the entire Sanhedrin" (ibid., p. 127).

[27] "I saw in the night visions, and behold, with the *clouds of heaven* there came one like a *son of man*. . . ."

[28] "The Lord says to my lord: 'Sit at *my right hand*, till I make your enemies your footstool.'" The "Son of man" motif (Mark 14:61b–62) was then crudely amalgamated with that from the "Suffering Servant" (= Mark 14:60–61a).

stand, we lack assurance not only that there had been a formal conviction of Jesus under Jewish law but also even a formal charge, not to mention an actual convening of the Sanhedrin—in short, we may doubt that there had ever ensued anything approaching a "trial" at all!

In light, then, of these four major considerations, even if we can agree with Fr. Brown's case for Jesus' arrest and interrogation by Jewish authorities, we must remain sensitive to the extraordinarily uncanny correspondence between what the Gospels *say* occurred and what happened to have been in the special interests of the Gospel writers decades later to *profess*, or to *believe*, or to *imagine* had occurred. Their renditions of Pilate's acquittal of Jesus served the self-protective needs of later Christian communities vis-à-vis Rome; and the traditions of a Jewish interrogation of Jesus *also* functioned literarily to move a now *condemned* Jesus along so that Pilate could soon thereafter acquit him. Additionally, the Gospel details of Jesus' demeanor and statements in the Sanhedrin resonate only too well with later Christian theology, and, in terms of origin, could well have been spawned by dependence upon Jewish Scriptural motifs.

These various possibilities suggest to me that, in reality, the Gospel writers knew only the most general progression of events (Jesus' capture, a rudimentary Jewish *interrogation* [not a "trial"], the handing of Jesus over to Rome, the crucifixion), but not the specifics of Jesus' last days, and that, to be exact, they may not even have been clear why, from the point of view of Jewish authorities, Jesus had to be arrested to begin with. On this last matter, the Evangelists would naturally have presumed that he had been deemed a "blasphemer" since this is surely how Christians were hearing *themselves* labeled by Jews of their own later day, who would have charged them with misconstruing a mere man as divine. As a specifically *religious* offense, blasphemy would also have been helpful to Christians in offsetting the more alarming *political* allegation that Jesus had fancied himself a would-be king.

Conditioned by these dynamics, the mind-set of the Gospel writers themselves would have come to contribute in a fundamental way to the defamation of Jewish elements as callous, even evil.

C. "Responsibility" in Later Time Frames

Accordingly, beyond Fr. Brown's question of the "responsibility" which may be assigned to some first-century contemporaries of Jesus—be they Jewish or Roman—there surface other questions of consequence on this matter: the responsibility of the *Gospel writers* for disseminating interpretations maligning the entire Jewish people, and, more far-reaching still, the responsibility of *those who subsequently seized such texts as pretexts* for harming, even murdering, Jews who could not have borne the slightest connection to Jesus' death. Since Jews today are respectfully aware that Roman Catholics consider Jesus *the* Son of God, they do fully enough comprehend that what happened to Jesus became and remains a matter of the most profound consequence to Roman Catholics. But Jews would wish that Roman Catholics would reciprocate with *their* understanding that it is the Jewish view that (1) Jesus was *a* son of God in the same sense that we are all offspring of God; and thus that (2) *all* unjust killings of human beings (that of Jesus among them) may be *commensurate* one with another; that (3) these also include the unjust deaths of countless Jews over the centuries for the sole reason that they were vilified as "Christ-killers"[29]; and that (4) *their* deaths may have been even more unwarranted than that of Jesus given that *he* opted for a course that portended risk of arrest, even of execution, while these later Jews died only as an indirect consequence of *his* decision, not their own. In these matters, also of the most profound consequence, there should likewise reverberate Fr. Brown's quest to trace and determine responsibility!

---

[29] Cf. Brown on Jeremiah (*Death*, p. 396). Only if Jeremiah had become deemed founder of, or co-opted by, *another* religion might Jews have been blamed by the new religionists for abusing him. In this sense, since it was Christians who took Jesus the Jew and made him into a Christian, *Christians* would in some sense be responsible for the "Christ-killer" allegation (rather than Jews being guilty of it).

The reasons these matters are so vital to Jews can also be conveyed anecdotally. For example:

• The crucifixion conjures up for some Jews medieval images
of two women[30] stationed beneath the cross (Figure 1[31]) and rep-
resenting the Church (on *Jesus'* right) and the blindfolded Synagogue (on *Jesus'* left[32]). Here, as if to dramatize the Synagogue's
opaqueness, she may be shown in her blind(folded)ness breaking
her staff as she wields it in piercing the Lamb of God. The message
conveyed would be that the deicidal Jews, in and *by* their blind-
ness, have murdered Christ, but the Church has readily accepted,
in his spurting blood, her commission of his authority at his very
moment of expiration (Figure 2[33]).

Sometimes the Synagogue is being vengefully stabbed through
the top of her head or through the back of her neck by a daggered
hand extruding from the end of a so-called "living" cross (Figure
3[34]).

• For Jews, Jesus on the cross also conjures up images of Cru-
sader armies trekking through Europe to recapture Jerusalem
from the Moslem "infidel," and justifying their murder of Jews
en route by appeals to the Gospels' own assessments of Jews as
murderers of Jesus and infidels themselves! Other pogroms (mas-
sacres of Jews) were triggered by outrageous "blood libels" to the
effect that Jews were regularly re-enacting their execution of Jesus
by kidnaping Christian children to secure blood Jews supposedly
needed to bake Passover *matzah*, unleavened bread (Figure 4).

---

[30] At this point in the program, slides were shown. The two women appear in
sculpture, manuscript illuminations, stained-glass windows, paintings, etc. See
Wolfgang Seiferth, *Synagoge und Kirche im Mittelalter* (Munich: Kösel-Verlag,
1964; trans. [Lee Chadeayne and Paul Gottwald] as *Synagogue and Church in the
Middle Ages: Two Symbols in Art and Literature* [New York: Frederick Ungar,
1970]); Gertrud Schiller, *Ikonographie der christlichen Kunst* (Gütersloh: Güter-
sloher Verlaghaus Gerd Mohn, 1966+; trans. [Janet Seligman] as *Iconography of
Christian Art* [Greenwich, Conn.: New York Graphic Society Ltd., 1971]), esp.
vol. 2: Plate ##364ff., 446ff., and 527ff.; Ruth Mellinkoff, *Outcasts: Signs of
Otherness in Northern European Art of the Late Middle Ages*, 2 vols. (Berkeley:
University of California Press, 1993); and Heinz Schreckenberg, *The Jews in
Christian Art: An Illustrated History* (New York: Continuum, 1996).
[31] Seiferth: #26.
[32] Given the Latin word for "left," the Synagogue would here (from Jesus'
vantage point) appear literally *sinister.*
[33] Seiferth: #18; Schreckenberg: p. 49 #27.
[34] Schreckenberg: p. 65 #2; Schiller 2: #527; cf. ## 529, 530, 531.

Figure 1. *Ecclesia* (Church) and *Synagoga* (Synagogue) Beneath the Cross (Medallion, ca. 1230; *Bibliothèque Nationale de France*, Paris)

• Jesus upon the cross also recalls depictions of Jews with swine faces at Jesus' trial, or with horns to link them to Satan (hence the grotesque *horned* hats by which Oberammergau used to costume priests and so-called "rabbis" of the Sanhedrin (Figure 5).

• Speaking once again now of Oberammergau, not even Krauskopf could have anticipated, let alone imagined, how a Hitler would employ this play to indoctrinate the SS[35] by capitalizing on Christian supersessionist theology: the conviction that, precisely since "the Jews" had killed Jesus, Gentiles had replaced them as the chosen people—suggesting, in turn, that persistence of Jews into the twentieth century was an anomaly, a quirk or mistake of history (since Jews were fossils meant to have disappeared far earlier).[36]

---

[35] Hitler attended the last performance of 1930, and also on August 13, 1934 (although the play is customarily presented only in years ending in zero, special showings were held in 1934, the 300th anniversary of its original production).

[36] Hitler classified the play a racially important cultural document (*"Anschaung-*

Figure 2. Blindfolded *Synagoga* (Synagogue) Breaking Staff by Piercing Christ; *Ecclesia* (Church) Receiving the Resulting Flow of His Blood. (Missal illustration, before 1250; Walters Art Gallery, Baltimore [Mr. & Mrs. Philip Hofer collection])

• A depiction five centuries previous to Hitler portrays the Church as presiding over the Synagogue's burial already during Jesus' day (Figure 6[37]). Any notion of the Synagogue as having died *long ago* could well have lessened resistance to Hitler's efforts to exterminate them: if Jews were already supposed to have disappeared, why not look the other way if that process was being belatedly completed *now*?

---

sunterricht für Rassenunterschiede" [literally, "an instruction for racial distinction"]; see *Allgemeine Jüdische Wochenzeitung* [June 6, 1980]) for "never has the menace of Jewry been so convincingly portrayed" (*Hitler's Secret Conversations, 1941– 1944* [New York: Octagon, 1972], p. 457). Centuries of performances may have *predisposed* Oberammergau's populace toward National Socialism: about 60% were active Nazis during the 1930s (at one point, nine of the production's ten major actors—the exception playing "Judas"—were party members; cf. P. Baum, "Background of the Oberammergau Passion Play" [American Jewish Congress release (November 7, 1966), p. 3]).
    [37] Schreckenberg: p. 57 #8; Seiferth: #52.

Figure 3. *Synagoga* (Synagogue) Stabbed by Daggered-Hand from Living Cross (Wall painting by Giovanni da Modena; Bologna, S. Petronio, chapel of S. Giorgio; ca. 1410–20)

- Hauntingly, almost eight centuries (ca. 1160) before the ovens of Auschwitz, an artist etched into a silver paten[38] images of infidel Jews queuing up behind a banner of the Synagogue to march into a blazing *oven*; the interpretative inscription running along the rim avers that the Synagogue deserves (the fires of) hell for rejecting Christ (*que reprobat Xr[istu]m Sinagoga meretur abissum*).[39]
- Even in the present decade, Radio City's 1993 passion drama, "Jesus Was His Name,"[40] touring some thirty American cities and

---

[38] Seiferth: #21.

[39] Can we not help but recall, in this regard, Matthew 25:41: "He will say to those at his *left*, 'Depart from me, you cursed, into the eternal *fire* . . .' "?

[40] Created by Robert Hossein; adapted by Alain Decaux; produced by Eliot Weisman, Eric Weisman, and Levoy Sayan.

Figure 4. Jews Taking Blood from Christian Children, for Their Mystic Rites (from *Book of the Cabala of Abraham the Jew* [Library of the Arsenal, Paris]; used here on the cover of *The Blood Libel Legend: a Casebook in Anti-Semitic Folklore*, ed. by Alan Dundes [Madison: U. of Wisconsin, 1991])

Figure 5. Sanhedrin Priests and "Rabbis" Wearing Horns (Oberammergau Passion Play, 1980)

billing itself "a message of love," costumed the Jewish arresting party in Darth Vader-style uniforms and headgear (Figure 7), with death-masks (Figure 8) accompanied by snakelike hissing sounds adorning the Jewish high priest Caiaphas and his fellow Sanhedrin judges! Protests halted the New York production several days until less offensive raiment could be substituted. While the play died out prematurely, ironically in *Bethlehem* (Pennsylvania), the memories it imprinted remain to torment nonetheless.

CONCLUSION

Jews will never successfully parry this problem of dealing with responsibility for Jesus' death until most can forthrightly address the issues involved and frame necessary guidelines. For Jews simply to respond on the level of "the *Romans* did it" is neither nuanced nor sophisticated, nor fully accurate. It is certainly not congruent with a people priding themselves on knowledge. We simply must be willing to acknowledge that it is not at all impossi-

Figure 6. *Ecclesia* [Church] Presides Over *Synagoga's* [Synagogue's] Burial (*Bibliothèque Nationale de France*, Paris; ca. 1410)

Figure 7. Jewish Arresting Party in Darth Vader-style Uniforms and Headgear (Radio City Music Hall's "Jesus Was His Name" [1993])

ble that some Jewish leaders recommended the death of Jesus to Pilate. We must also recognize why it is that we have been so averse to saying this even to ourselves: because "so total has been the charge against us that we have been constrained to make a total denial."[41]

Once we achieve this admission, other emphases will come into sharper focus. Without denying any nobility of Jesus' mission, we must be able to verbalize that responsibility for his death lies also with *Jesus himself* (who must have anticipated the possibility of execution); that given the seemingly threatening nature of Jesus' preachment, honest, even righteous persons may have been among those sincerely convinced that his death was not only necessary but deserved[42]; that the reason the death of Jesus (as opposed to that of other Jews) has been so uniquely important is

---

[41] Sandmel, *We Jews and Jesus* (New York: Oxford, 1965), p. 141.

[42] "It is not in the least impossible that the Jewish national officials . . . sought the death of Jesus . . . because they actually believed, as . . . John [11:50] suggests, that the death of one man might avert political disaster for the whole nation" (Wilson, *Execution*, pp. 172ff.).

Figure 8. Caiaphas' Death-mask Accompanied by Snake-like Hissing Sounds (Radio City Music Hall's "Jesus Was His Name" [1993])

that he was proclaimed divine by elements who not only removed him from Judaism but also became antithetical to the Jewish people; that the portraits of Jesus' life which congealed in the Gospels became skewed by the theological presuppositions of developing Christian theology and by the animosities of Evangelists in their own day, and in terms of accuracy as history are now questionable on many bases; that in the Jewish view the unwarranted execution or killing of *any* other righteous person becomes a tragedy possibly commensurate with the death of Jesus himself; and thus, in connection with the subject of Jesus' execution, responsibility for some such deaths may adhere not only to the Gospel writers themselves but also—indeed, even more so—to those who later used Gospel texts as pretexts for murdering Jews.

It is also legitimate for Jews to ask: If we are to speak of Jesus' death, why must we focus only on persons from the past—whom we do not know and about whom we can do nothing—when we *can* also inquire whether today's Christians are able to comprehend and derive spiritual profit from their own scriptures without depending any longer upon feelings of hostility for the furtherance of their religion. In consonance with Jesus' own teachings, can the Gospel passion traditions somehow quiet destructive impulses, foster mutual sympathy and understanding, and offer an ideal for human life? If not, then the irony emerges that, so long as Jews are maligned as "Christ-killers," they will feel that their accusers are assuming the same kind of unjust prosecutorial role vis-à-vis *the Jewish people* that the Gospels customarily assign to the Sanhedrin vis-à-vis Jesus.[43]

Burton Visotzky: I am a little breathless from the impressive presentations of each scholar. In a very limited period of time, they have managed to draw very carefully for us not only the common ground, but the problem that we share in this room tonight. I do want to remark on a phenomenon that occurred tonight here at Fordham, a Jesuit University. In this room where Jews and Christians sit together, you heard one, and I will add my voice to it, a second rabbi, assent to Fr. Brown's characterization that there most likely was some Jewish involvement in the death of Jesus. Back when I was a kid riding my bike in the schoolyard of Saint Tim's, the only Jew who would say this out loud was Lenny Bruce. It was nothing more and nothing less than the subject of comedy to think that a Jew—that soon after the Holo-

---

[43] Thus, ironically, can Jesus-on-the-cross indeed become a symbol of the maltreatment of his fellow-Jewish people!

caust—could say out loud that our ancestors might have had some hand in it. But we have come a long way since then. I want briefly to lay out the problem to which Dr. Cook and Fr. Brown alluded, and I want to do it by opening with a question to my rabbinical colleague, Dr. Cook.

When I was in Warsaw this summer, I had the opportunity to meet Jews and Christians who were there for the sole purpose of talking to one another. There were Jews who were old enough still to have numbers tattooed on their arms, and there were Christians who spoke German and Polish, and who were old enough for us to know better than to ask what they did during World War Two.

I was struck mostly, though, by a young Catholic Pole in his early twenties who served as a volunteer at Auschwitz. He gave guided tours of Auschwitz so that Poles and Germans and other visitors would remember the horrors that the Nazis had brought to the Jews. But he was distressed at the time of this dialogue. He was distressed because he had trouble finding Jewish partners in Poland with whom to have dialogue. Now it certainly was not necessary to point out to him that one of the reasons there were very few Jewish partners with whom to have dialogue was that the Nazis had, in large part, succeeded in making Poland free of Jews. But he lamented that in the Jewish community of Poland, small as it was, and even in the broader Jewish community, it was very hard to find Jews who would talk to Catholics about what they had in common.

Rabbi Cook, I think that you have answered that Polish Catholic's question in spades tonight with the tail end of your talk, both before and during your slide presentation. We Jews carry a great deal of wounding and hurt, and yet we are here because we feel some need to talk. What I want to know is: if we accept some culpability, what do we do with it? How do we get past the two thousand years of history that have intervened and treated Jews so miserably? How do we let Christians off the hook for the guilt they bear? And, what do we owe to Christians in engaging them in dialogue? Finally, what do we Jews who participate in these kind of forums have to worry about? To what are we exposing ourselves? What should we be fearing?

Michael Cook: It may be suitable to begin with a parable from ancient rabbinic writings, in a body of literature called the *Tosephta* (tractate Sanhedrin 9:7, a passage commenting on Deuteronomy 21:23 ["he who is hanged is a reproach to God"]). It tells of identical-twin brothers. One became king of the universe and the other an ordinary thief. The latter was eventually caught and crucified. Passers-by, glancing at the thief on the cross, noted his striking resemblance to the king of the universe. They reacted: "It seems as if *the king of the universe* is being crucified!"

One meaning of the parable is as follows: The human being is created in God's image. Accordingly, when any human being is put to death, it appears as if God personally is being executed. This constitutes a reproach to God and as such is tragic beyond comprehension.

An application of this parable to your question would be as follows: If Jews today felt truly free to discuss the execution of Jesus, they would likely pronounce it as tragic as, possibly, they would that of any other person. This would certainly be true in the case of Jesus, unique in the very least because of his impact upon history. I believe that Jews would actually feel *unburdened* to view and to express the death of Jesus as a tragedy.

With regard, however, to your word "culpability," I have learned from Raymond Brown that "culpability" is not the best term. Instead, he has employed the word "responsibility," and has remained remarkably free from any terminology of *blame*.

Respecting, then, *"responsibility"* for Jesus' execution, Jews would, I think, become open to accepting or acknowledging the possible responsibility by *some* first-century Jews as long as that acknowledgment would not become enlisted against the Jewish people as a whole. Being realistic, I must say that I am not sure that the Jewish community is ready, or will be ready for generations, to feel comfortable acknowledging possible involvement of *any* Jewish officials in the death of Jesus precisely because of this fear that such acknowledgment will still end up being wielded against "the Jews" as a people.

I know a woman who used to go to Miami University in Oxford, Ohio. She was awakened once in 1965 at two o'clock in the morning by someone across the hall who had just heard on television that the Second Vatican Council, in its Declaration on

Non-Christian Religions, no longer held all Jews responsible (as a matter of fact, the word actually used in the Declaration was "blamed") for Jesus' death—not *all* the Jews of Jesus' day nor *any* of those of *later* times. This person could not wait to awaken my friend to tell her that she was now freed of all responsibility. Of course, my friend had never felt responsible to start with. Moreover, I am certain that she would have preferred to have been left undisturbed!

Burton Visotzky: Both presenters share a very clear notion of how to sketch the death of Jesus in what I will term four different eras. The first era is the actual event itself. That is to say, sometime in the thirties in Palestine of the first century, Jesus was put to death and some Jews may have had some responsibility *even though* it was the Romans per se who crucified him. The next era is the New Testament era. Within a century after Jesus' death, and for a variety of reasons sketched by both Fr. Brown and Rabbi Cook, Gospel accounts did their presentation of the death of Jesus. A third era which was alluded to was from the beginnings of the church fathers all the way up to the Holocaust. That is the era of the church blaming the Jews for deicide and persecuting the Jews as a result. The last era is the one we are blessedly living in and watching unfold before our very eyes, and it is the post-Vatican II era.

When I was talking with Ray Brown to prepare for this evening, I, who studied the church fathers, said to him, "Ray, what are you going to do with the church fathers? I know you are a New Testament scholar but I can guarantee you we Jews are going to ask you about the church fathers." Fr. Brown responded by saying that Vatican II deliberately contradicts the church fathers.

I think that is a terribly important point to realize. *Nostra Aetate*, "in our times": our times are really extraordinary! Two thousand years of church teaching have been overturned. And whether it is the Holocaust that was the cause, or the enlightenment of the church, or the outcries of Jews, is almost incidental. We are in a new era, an era of ease and scholarship, so that Jews and Christians can share a common view (with the necessary nuances) from their differing perspectives. Now having said that, and having said that

I read those 1,600 pages of your *Death of the Messiah* and found your view persuasive, I nevertheless have a nagging doubt, just as my colleague Michael Cook does. How will your words be heard, Fr. Brown? How will your words be heard when you, the incredibly careful scholar that you are, write that some Jews were in some degree and way responsible for the death of Christ? How do the Catholic boys at Saint Tim's hear what you say? How do the skinheads hear what you say? How do mainline Protestants and Catholics hear what you say? How do you address Jewish fears? Where is your responsibility both as a priest and a scholar to find what you think is the historic event and yet address the current era of *Nostra Aetate*?

Raymond Brown: Well, I will tell you what I do. I read the Gospel passages every Lent, particularly John's Gospel passages. Before I read them, I remind people of some of the things I have said tonight, that these tendencies have developed beyond what happened in the liturgies. I develop very much the history of the polemic with the synagogue, and that these polemics reflect Jewish–Christian relations of the 80s and the 90s of the first century. I remind them that in subsequent centuries these passages produced intense dislike of Jews. I ask people when they listen to these Gospel passages to have that in mind, and to ask themselves whether they can possibly take those passages as anti-Jewish, without listening to the kind of thing that Vatican II said. It was the intention of Vatican II to modify that kind of tendency to universalize and generalize negatively about all Jews.

I ask them, therefore, to enter into debate, with responsible listening to the scriptures, and realizing that every document is written by human beings conditioned by certain situations, and that to get to the message you are going to make an enormous mistake if you overlook the condition. Therefore, I use it as a chance to educate Christian people about the problems that those passages have wrought.

I have told generations of seminarians that it is utterly irresponsible to simply read those passages aloud and let them hang there without commenting on them. Now, I have resisted all my life another, easier route of not reading them—as if they never existed. I do not think we help our problems if we pretend they are not there. They *are* there and we have to deal with them. But I encourage responsive healing.

Burton Visotzky: I think that we have been given a great advantage because both Fr. Brown and Rabbi Cook, in addition to being extraordinary scholars, are intimately involved in the life of church and synagogue. Fr. Brown, when he lived in New York City, used to serve mass at Corpus Christi and read on Sunday. In addition to teaching his Catholic disciples he also taught at Union Theological Seminary, a Protestant seminary. Rabbi Cook has served in congregations. Now at Hebrew Union College in Cincinnati, he not only teaches New Testament to Reform rabbis, but also teaches them homiletics, how to preach. So both of them in their work and life have continued to advance the dialogue.

Audience member: What is the quality of New Testament evidence about the crucifixion? For example, is the evidence strong about Barabbas?

Raymond Brown: Inevitably there are historical problems with the Gospel account. I spend a great deal of time talking about the problem of Barabbas and the lack of evidence of releasing a criminal every year. I agree totally with the lack of evidence. In my judgment, a Jewish criminal named Barabbas was probably released, but it was brought into juxtaposition with the crucifixion of Jesus and with Jews polemically, as: look, a criminal was released and an innocent man put to death. It is just the development I have talked about regarding polemicization and generalization, so I certainly agree that went on.

I have to be more careful, though, in terms of historic retrojection because, for instance, Paul's statement about the Jews killing the Lord Jesus is done long before the Jewish revolt, and has no possible tone of relieving Romans from the problem. Therefore, I am convinced that the picture of Jewish involvement in the death of Jesus is strongly in place and preached without the subsequent polemic (which was true and inevitable), dealing with sensitivity about Roman involvement with the crucifixion.

Basically, if someone said to me, do you think that the Gospel picture is historical?, I am willing to settle for Josephus' picture.

Since Josephus is Jewish, it certainly has nothing to do with some of the issues that have been raised. Josephus says: "although Pilate condemned him to the cross upon the indictment of the first ranking men among us." I think that Josephus actually wrote that, and he is a *Jewish* historian. One thing that I think will help us is the realization that the current position describing Roman responsibility now gets a bit more problematic if Jewish involvement is recognized. I think Romans were responsible. Still, *pure* Roman responsibility is insufficient without there being important Jewish involvement. This became a standard Jewish presentation only in the last two centuries. I think up to 1800 not a single Jew could be quoted as saying the Romans did it. In fact, Jews in Europe insisted that the Jewish evidence was: No, we did this and Jesus deserved it. Now I am not saying that is historical at all, but I am pointing out that it is helpful for Jews to know that often what they have been taught in synagogue or Sunday schools is of fairly recent origin. That does not mean necessarily it is wrong. This historic reconstruction develops as the New Testament is more critically studied. But still, it is, in a sense, a recent issue in the long debate about the Jews and Christians.

Audience member: I see a road to reconciliation that has not been mentioned. In Christian exegesis of the Old Testament, particularly of Isaiah, the historical inevitability of the death of Jesus, in order to bring about the world-to-come and to take on the sins of the world, is *foreordained*. How can Jews have responsibility for something that Christians themselves say was inevitable?

Michael Cook: To rephrase your question: "If Isaiah predicts the necessity of Jesus' dying, then why should Jews be held *responsible* for his execution when they were only a cog in the machinery effecting humanity's salvation?"

Judaism does *not* interpret Isaiah as predictive of the coming of Jesus. In the Jewish view, Jesus is neither mentioned nor predicted anywhere in the Jewish Bible. (Whether the *Messiah* is predicted is a different issue.) One of the areas where I diverge somewhat from Fr. Brown is that I believe that a larger number of the events in Jesus' life were accommodated, were *matched*, to Jewish scriptural themes rather than that Jesus' life *reminded* Christians of these themes. Respecting your specific question, I believe that Jesus' image was largely *framed* in the light, e.g., of Isaiah 53, not that Isaiah 53 predicted the life or death of Jesus.

An implication of your question is very interesting. What you ask respecting the responsibility of "the Jews" could just as well be asked concerning *Judas*: why should Judas be vilified when he too was only doing what was necessary—when he also was a vital cog in machinery effecting humanity's salvation (since it was his act of betrayal that set into motion Jesus' saving death)? Such a question seems especially apt since "Jew" and "Judas" are virtually the same word in Greek as well as Hebrew, even suggesting that some equation of "Jews" and "Judas" may have been intended by the Gospel writers themselves.

When Jesus is held to say in Mark 14:21, "The Son of man goes as it is written of him, but woe to that man [= the Jews?] by whom the Son of man is betrayed," that answer constitutes a virtual parallel to your question about the *Jews*. On the one hand, the question about Judas could be answered: Yes, Jesus had to die, but woe to *heinous* Judas who need not himself have opted to betray him (he was, in other words, not a blind instrument of fate). On the other hand, this *same* answer could then be applied to the Jews by the following reasoning: Yes, Jesus had to die, but woe to those *heinous* Jews who need not themselves have opted to condemn him! Granted, what happened to Jesus was divinely ordained, but the crime which Jews *of their own accord* chose to commit was entirely without Divine sanction. As such, Jews would remain a truly *guilty* party.

In light of this kind of argument, Jews would *still* be regarded as "responsible" (*blameworthy*, in the Gospels' view) *even if* what they did was deemed necessary for the salvation of humanity.

Audience member: How would the Gospels be heard by Roman Catholics, given Fr. Brown's interpretation? You have earlier spoken of the tendency for preachers to simplify when accounting for what happened in the Gospels. Is it realistic to imagine that the kind of nuance and explication of the Gospels offered by Fr. Brown can ever prevail throughout the world?

Michael Cook: The question asks how realistic is the potential for dissemination, and acceptance, of Fr. Brown's nuanced approach. This concern is extraordinarily on the mark. Essentially, what this boils down to is whether *laypeople* can be effectively brought into the arena of learned Jewish-Christian dialogue.

Ever since the promulgation of *Nostra Aetate*, we have made marvelous progress in understanding when it comes to dialogue between and among *academicians*, also among *clergy*. The number of academic and clergy symposia sponsored has been legion! But our task in the 1990s, it seems to me, now requires that we turn our *primary* attention to our *laities*—such as we are today doing in this symposium here at Fordham. I am very concerned with the current circumstance wherein Christian–Jewish dialogue elsewhere seems to be operating the *least* among the persons whose participation we need the *most*.

This relative non-involvement of our laities in Christian-Jewish dialogue reminds me of a lion in Brooklyn, back in the 1940s, who escaped from his circus cage. The keepers located him next morning, but, strangely enough, he had only gone several blocks, stopping at an abandoned house with a thirty-foot strand of fence in front of it. There was the lion, pacing back and forth before that fence, continuing that same monotonous yet comfortable habit of lateral movement into which he had been born in a circus cage, free and yet at the same time not entirely free after all. For whenever he would reach a corner, at one end of the fence, he would simply reverse his direction. Having broken out of one cage, he had become complacent with another, and simply could not bring himself to turn that corner!

It was likewise several decades ago that we Christians and Jews appeared to break out of our own patterns of enshacklement vis-à-vis each other, leaving them, so we may have thought, far behind us. Are most Christians and Jews today likewise engaged in lateral pacing before a fence whose corner we are hesitant to turn, a corner concerning which there is no getting around that we are not getting around? The challenge for all of us in the 90s, so it seems to me, is to shift our progress in Christian-Jewish relations into the lay arena, where it most properly belongs, and to cope with the factors obstructing this shift.

To apply this to your question, the relative *exclusion* of the laity from involvement in study and knowledgeable interfaith discourse will *impede* the successful dissemination of—and, I feel, *apprehension* and *comprehension* of—Fr. Brown's nuanced approach and presentation. I therefore think your question is of the most profound significance.

Audience member: Were the Pharisees of Jesus' time the fore-runners of the rabbis of the second century and later?

Raymond Brown: What the Pharisees were in Jesus' time and what the rabbis were in the second century is not as simple a relationship as people might think. I think only six people were ever called Pharisees *by name* in all of the documentation. It is a very low number. And one person who says he was a Pharisee, and a very firm Pharisee, persecuted Christians and tried to get rid of them. That is Saul of Tarsus. So there are reasons why the Pharisees' relationship to Jesus may have been far more compli-cated than we have assumed.

Let us turn it around. You have asked me a question: How many priests will listen to this? But still you also have a whole papal document and a conciliar document. Also, in his latest writ-ings Pope John Paul II shows a remarkable sensitivity on some of these issues and that tells people they must change their mind.

I do not think there can be similar kinds of statements within Judaism, and I guess there is a complicated relationship between the involvement of Jewish authorities and later Gospel scripture. How many rabbis are going to tell their people that, if they are told by Rabbi Cook or Rabbi Visotzky? How many of them will take the trouble to communicate a very complicated picture in the synagogue when it is easier to communicate simplification? So we have difficulty on *both* sides of that picture. How do you get your clergy, who have an easier time by presenting a simpli-fied, if a somewhat distorted picture, instead to present a nuanced picture which will have to make people think?

Michael Cook: To be fair, dialogue also needs to be *balanced*. The problem with which Fr. Brown has so earnestly tried to wrestle has a counterpart within the Jewish experience—and to be fair and balanced I feel that this counterpart should be noted now.

While ancient rabbinic literature does not often mention Jesus or Christianity, the relatively few allusions there are do indeed tend to be disparaging. Have Jews, then, addressed the problem of how to deal with anti-Christian material in rabbinic literature (a task ostensibly analogous to the challenge that Christians should now address regarding anti-Jewish material in the New Testament)? The answer is no. Jews to this day have generally not been drawn to address this problem.

Reasons are not hard to fathom: (1) Rabbinic literature has never been broadly influential in European or American societies—that is, it has never occupied a position of any predominance in social settings where Christianity has been a *minority* vulnerable to denigration. So even though their own literature has in this one respect been biased, Jews have had the "luxury" of not having to redress this kind of problem. (2) Jews have, of course, also been *unmotivated* to address the issue, this given their resentment over the history of the persecution they feel they have received at Christian hands. (3) The very presence of negativity toward the figure of Jesus in rabbinic literature begs the extremely important question of whether the rabbis were not *responding* to start with to the negative picture of the *Jews* in the Gospels, and to a Jesus who is cast as espousing it. I feel we should not undervalue the significance of that consideration.

Now with respect to the *Pharisees*, we should not get the impression from Fr. Brown that, since Paul was a Pharisee and persecuted Christianity, all Gospel passages showing Pharisees harassing Jesus are therefore credible. This would be an unwarranted and false conclusion. In my view, many Gospel passages casting the Pharisees as enemies of Jesus reflect the hostility suffusing later decades of the first century retrojected and superimposed upon the time of Jesus' ministry.

I am not one of those who insist that Jesus himself had to be a Pharisee. But I do feel that it is fair to keep in mind the existence of some commonalities between the Pharisees and Jesus: that when Jesus is asked (in Mark 12 and parallels) to identify the greatest teaching, his answers—the *Sh'ma* and the Golden Rule— are certainly traditions to which the Pharisees themselves would have subscribed. Moreover, teaching in the form of parables, especially the parables of the coming of the Kingdom of God, was typical of the Pharisees. Then there is the striking resemblance between the Lord's Prayer and what came to be known in Jewish liturgy as the *Qaddish*. All these and many other examples are illustrative of emphases shared between Jesus and the Pharisees. The latter thus emerge as far removed from what (in direct dependence upon the Gospels) used to be the primary definition of the Pharisees as "hypocrites." That kind of mentality, that the Pharisees are to be equated with hypocrisy, is something we definitely have to put to rest.

Catholic-Jewish Dialogue and the New Millenium

November 20, 1995

Margaret Steinfels: Tonight's dialogue is the third in this series and it continues a tradition established by the conference held at Fordham in 1990, which was the twenty-fifth anniversary of *Nostra Aetate*'s promulgation at the closing session of the Second Vatican Council in 1965. Tonight our distinguished speakers continue this conversation on the thirtieth anniversary of *Nostra Aetate*, which most of you know is the Declaration on the Relationship of the Church to Non-Christian Religions.

This year is also the thirtieth anniversary of a closely related Vatican II document, *Dignitatis Humanae*, the Declaration on Religious Liberty, one of whose chief framers was John Courtney Murray, S.J., a member of the Jesuit community that has built and sustained this great university. The subtitle of that Declaration on Religious Liberty reads: On the Rights of the Person and Communities to Social and Civil Liberty in Religious Matters. Thirty years ago those words signaled an important shift in the Catholic Church's understanding of the dignity of the human person in matters of religious faith, religious community, and religious liberty. This shift was also clearly marked in *Nostra Aetate*, whose opening words speak of humankind drawing more closely together and of the bonds of friendship between different peoples being strengthened. These words, little more than a hope in 1965, are now a reality everywhere in our society and in our culture, and they are embodied in tonight's dialogue. Our two speakers, as leaders of their religious communities, contributed greatly to building these bonds. Neither is planning to speak infallibly, so each of them may want to respond directly to the other's comments.

Ismar Schorsch: Cardinal O'Connor, Fr. O'Hare, Ms. Steinfels, ladies and gentlemen, in my community it is very difficult to speak with infallibility. In case you do not believe me, let me remind you of a story that is worth repeating. I tell you this story in part because Cardinal O'Connor was an admiral in the Navy a few years ago. The story is told that a yeshiva in Boston, a Jewish academy of higher learning, had a rather progressive president and he decided that it would be good for his young men if they did some exercising. So he called in one of his more muscular teachers and he said, "I would like you to build a rowing team. Take out our boys every afternoon on the Charles River and row with them." The teacher, dutifully, rowed every day with the best student athletes he could find.

After several months, they entered their first race and they came in last. So the president of the yeshiva was rather distressed. He called in the coach and he said, "I would like you to go to Harvard and see what they did. They came in first." The coach did so, and a couple of days later he came back and his president asked him what he had learned. The coach said, "It is remarkable. They do things differently at Harvard. There are eight men per row and only one shouts." So I present myself here, Cardinal O'Connor, in the modest role of just one of the coxswains of the Jewish boat.

Nostra Aetate was a turning point in Jewish-Catholic relations. It occurred thirty years ago. We can also look at it in reference to the Holocaust, and that is where I would like to begin. In 1965, twenty years after the Holocaust, the Declaration on the Relationship of the Church to Non-Christian Religions was not uninfluenced by the lessons of the Holocaust. So permit me to begin with a brief historical survey that I think sets the tone for the watershed of *Nostra Aetate*.

On January 14, 1933, sixteen days before Hitler became Chancellor, there was a dialogue, perhaps not unlike this dialogue, in Stuttgart, at the Academy for Jewish Learning, the Lehrhaus. This dialogue was between one of the well-known, progressive, Protestant academics, Karl Ludwig Schmidt, and the well-known Jewish philosopher Martin Buber. They dialogued about the differences between Judaism and Christianity and they titled their dialogue, "Church, State, Nation and the Jewish People."[1]

---

[1] See Paul R. Mendes-Flohr, "Ambivalent Dialogue: Jewish-Christian Theo-

At the heart of this dialogue was the difference in the Jewish and Christian conceptions of the Messiah. This is the way Buber articulated the agenda of the discussion: "If we wish to reduce the schism between Jews and Christians, between Israel and the Church, to a formula, we can say, the Church stands on the belief in the having come of Christ as the God-given redemption of man. We, Israel, are incapable of believing this. The Church views our declaration either as a case of not wanting to believe, as a grave sort of obduracy, or as a kind of curse, as a basic limitation on the ability to recognize reality, as the blinding of Israel, which prevents it from seeing the light."

Toward the end of this dialogue Martin Buber took the audience to the medieval town of Worms in the Rhineland. It was a town that Buber was very fond of visiting. In the heart of that old medieval town there is a magnificent cathedral, and not far from the cathedral is one of the very largest Jewish cemeteries in Europe, a cemetery whose graves go all the way back to the eleventh and twelfth centuries. Buber compared this magnificent cathedral to the disordered, shabby state of this immense Jewish cemetery. He marveled at the manner in which the cathedral asserted its prominence in the world and then he commented on the disheveled state of the Jewish cemetery. Buber affirmed that all of the suffering, all of the pain that lay in that cemetery, a reflection of the Jewish historical experience, was his experience. That cemetery may have consisted of broken tombstones and a lot of ashes, but that cemetery was his religion, and God's covenant with that religion had not been broken. It still held firm, and Buber still continued to avow it.

I take you back to that debate not because of the issue between them but because of what was not said. This was but sixteen days before Hitler was to assume the Chancellorship of Germany, to take Germany down the abysmal road of self-destruction. There was not a word spoken in that dialogue about the contemporary situation. Nothing was said about the vulgarity of Nazi anti-Semitism, about its unremitting assault upon the dignity of the Jews

logical Encounter in the Weimar Republic," In *Judaism and Christianity Under the Impact of National Socialism*, ed. Otto Dov Kulka and Paul Mendes-Flohr (Jerusalem: Historical Society of Israel, 1987), pp. 122–32.

and Judaism. Hitler was about to become the Chancellor of Germany and there was no word of compassion, no awareness that the moral collapse of a great nation-state was about to begin.

That debate was a tragedy, a religious and moral tragedy. For it was divorced from the catastrophe about to strike Germany and its Jews. I say this with high regard for Professor Schmidt, for he lost his job when the Nazis came to power. In 1933, he was dismissed along with all the other unacceptable academics and civil servants in the German bureaucracy. The Nazis cleaned house. And he went to Basel. He survived the Nazi debacle. He did not die until 1956. Yet even this progressive, Protestant academic could not bring himself to face the unremitting Nazi onslaught on Jews and Judaism.

That is a story that suggests the tragedy to come. It took but a small minority of radical anti-Semites, of racial anti-Semites, of secular anti-Christian, anti-Jewish anti-Semites to eradicate European Jewry. But the perpetrators needed the quiet indifference of the bystanders. The reason the bystanders did not raise their voice in protest is because of a long tradition of contempt for Judaism. It was the traditional anti-Semitism of the Church that silenced the voice of the bystanders and made it possible for the radical anti-Semites to realize their dream of a Europe that would be *Judenrein*.

Vatican II and its declaration on the Jews must be appreciated against that backdrop, against the bankruptcy of the traditional houses of worship in the face of the most determined, ferocious assault on any minority in European history. There was a pervasive sense of unease in Protestant and Catholic circles after the Second World War. It was that unease which prompted Pope John XXIII not only to convene Vatican II but also to push the Council in the direction of a new relationship between Judaism and Christianity. As you well know, it was Augustin Cardinal Bea who was the spearhead of this Declaration on the Jews and other non-Catholics. I might observe that one of the Jewish spokesmen who was intimately involved in preparing the declaration, in advocating the declaration, in lobbying for the declaration, was Abraham Joshua Heschel, who taught for many years at the Jewish Theological Seminary. Professor Heschel met with Pope John XXIII. He met with Cardinal Bea. I will read to you just one passage that Professor Heschel wrote while lobbying for a liberal declaration on the Jews. I read it to you because of its uncanny relevance to the contemporary situation:

> It is such a situation that we face today when the survival of mankind, including its sacred legacy, is in balance. One wave of hatred, prejudice or contempt may bring in its wake the destruction of all mankind. Vicious deeds are but an aftermath of what is conceived in the hearts and minds of man. It is from the inner life of men and from the articulation of evil thoughts that evil actions take their rise. It is, therefore, of extreme importance that the sinfulness of thoughts and suspicion and hatred and particularly the sinfulness of any contemptuous utterance, however flippantly it is meant, be made clear to all mankind. This implies in particular to such thoughts and utterances about individuals or groups of other religions, races and nations. Speech has power and few men realize that words do not fade. What starts out as a sound, ends in a deed.[2]

Abraham Joshua Heschel was able to speak from deep, personal experience, for in 1933 he was in Germany. He worked closely with Martin Buber. He succeeded Buber when Buber left for Palestine in 1938. Heschel often said there was no one for us to call for help after 1933. We stood alone in the face of the Nazi onslaught. It was that sense of isolation that drove Heschel to become a leader in the civil rights movement, a leader in the anti-Vietnam War movement, a leader in the fight for a more liberal declaration on the part of the Catholic Church. Heschel wanted to overcome two millennia of teachings of contempt. Words have consequences. They did in the period of the Holocaust. They paralyzed people. People had been numbed and failed to realize the enormity of the actions being taken. So they did not protest.

That is the background of the Declaration in Vatican II and that Declaration began a new era, an era that assaulted the words in the Catholic tradition. As you well know, that Declaration acknowledged the debt of Christianity to Judaism. It cleared Jews of the charge of deicide. It gave no warrant for any kind of anti-Semitic teachings and it softened the impact of the universal mission of the Church.

---

[2] See Abraham Joshua Heschel, "What We Might Do Together," in *Moral Grandeur and Spiritual Audacity,* ed. Susannah Heschel (New York: Farrar, Straus & Giroux, 1996), pp. 299–300.

At the end of 1993 the Vatican recognized the State of Israel, another great forward step in the improvement of Catholic–Jewish ties. It was Cardinal O'Connor who labored hard and long behind the scenes to achieve the diplomatic ties between Israel and the Vatican. A little more than a year ago, on April 7, 1994, there was a Holocaust conference in the Vatican over which the Pope presided. At that Holocaust conference, which was attended by Holocaust survivors and leaders of the Jewish community, the Pope spoke with extraordinary compassion for the suffering the Jews experienced at the hands of the Nazis. Those two steps would not have come without the Declaration and Vatican II. So there is simply no doubt that a new era began exactly thirty years ago this fall.

Where do we go from here? I would like to suggest to you that the time has come to move beyond dialogue. The dialogue between Jews and Catholics has been constructive and wholesome and candid over the last thirty years. Many painful issues and disagreements have been talked through. I submit to you that it is time to move beyond the dialogue between the two of us to a common cause. That cause is the recognition of the weakening of the moral fiber of American society. That problem is well known and no one addressed it with more passion, fervor, and intensity than the Pope on his recent visit to the United States. It was a captivating performance, a challenge of the highest moral order. He compromised nowhere in the intellectual and religious demands that he made of Catholics and Americans who listened with such hunger for holiness.

There is a need to strengthen the moral fiber without destroying one of its great achievements, the separation of church and state. The public square in the United States consists of two domains. It consists of the state and it consists of society. We have protected the state from religious intrusion for the welfare and benefit of everyone, especially the minorities in America. What needs addressing, what needs enrichment and moral deepening is society, that public arena where we meet as groups and individuals, as Americans, to debate and labor for the welfare of the country as a whole. It is in that public arena, it seems to me, that we need to work as colleagues, Catholics and Jews, in order to enrich and sensitize our moral sensibilities.

There is an enormous amount of freedom in American society and I would submit to you that freedom for the individual is one of the great political achievements of Western history. One can plot the history of the United States in terms of the expansion of individual and group rights to disenfranchised minorities, from African-Americans to women, to gays and lesbians. This society has made a heroic effort to maximize the freedom of the individual and it has become, in consequence, the inspiration of the world. But that freedom comes with a recognition that we ought not to do everything that we are permitted to do, that we ought not to do everything that we are capable of doing. Where is that self-restraint going to come from?

It needs to come from intermediary institutions like the churches and the synagogues. Morality should not be legislated by the government. The job of the government is to interfere in our personal lives as little as possible. The job of the churches and the synagogues, the job of the neighborhoods and the clubs is to enable us to develop the moral integrity to use our freedoms with wisdom. To avoid self-destruction through excess that freedom must be offset, and restrained with civility. If we say everything that comes into our minds, we will not long be able to live together. It is not for the government to tell us what we may say or not. It is for the churches, it is for our conscience, it is for these intermediary institutions to sensitize us to the need for civility, self-restraint and mutual respect. I believe that is the glory of the American experiment, the tension between state and society. Religion belongs in society. It does not belong in the state because the state has a long history of violating the rights of minorities. Democracy is more than government by majority. Democracy is also a high degree of sensitivity for the rights of the minority.

I wish to conclude with a remarkable letter by Thomas Jefferson. In 1818 the leader of the Jewish community in the United States, Mordechai M. Noah, delivered a dedicatory address at the building of the new synagogue of Shearith Israel here in Manhattan. He sent that address to Thomas Jefferson. Thomas Jefferson dashed off one of those memorable notes that reverberates through the pages of American history:

> I thank you for the discourse on the consecration of the synagogue in your city with which you have been pleased to favor me. I have

read it with pleasure and instruction, having learned from it some valuable facts in Jewish history which I did not know before. Your sect, by its suffering has furnished proof of the universal spirit of religious intolerance inherent in every sect, disclaimed by all while feeble and practiced by all while in power. Our laws have applied the only antidote to this vice, protecting our religious as they do our civil rights by putting all, on an equal footing.[3]

John Cardinal O'Connor: Thank you, good friend Rabbi Schorsch. I am truly grateful to Fordham University—I say this with total sincerity—for sponsoring this symposium. My experience in engaging in the Jewish-Catholic dialogue throughout the United States and in some other parts of the world has been that what happens here in New York is quite different from what happens throughout the rest of the world. There is a vibrancy and a dynamism and I think that Fordham University helps to bring that into being.

I am reminded in this regard of a letter I received in the aftermath of Pope John Paul II's visit to New York, spoken of so eloquently by Rabbi Schorsch. I have received letters from people of every religious persuasion and of none. It has been a remarkable phenomenon. But one that touched me, and that I have shared with the Pope, came from a Jewish man who said: "I am the father of a daughter who has been very ill for a long time and I decided I was going to ask you to ask the Holy Father if he would pray for her. But I thought I would ask her first. So I asked her. I said, you understand what I am going to do. I am going to ask the Catholic Cardinal in New York to ask the Pope to pray for you, a Jewish girl. She thought for a moment and said, "that's O.K., this is New York." So this is O.K., it is Fordham University.

I was deeply touched, as were all of you, by Rabbi Schorsch's highly scholarly and profoundly sincere reflections. It is my own experience in the Catholic–Jewish dialogue that true dialogue is always highly personal. It is a risky venture in friendship. Indeed, if it is going to be constructive and meaningful, it must be felt

---

[3] Thomas Jefferson to Mordecai Manual Noah, May 28, 1818 in *Basic Writings of Thomas Jefferson*, ed. Philip S. Foner (New York: Willey Book Co., 1944), pp. 756–57.

very passionately. One has to risk being shaken to the roots of one's very being. Otherwise, again my personal experience, what we call dialogue so easily can be simply the equivalent of cocktail chatter. Cocktail chatter can sometimes be coldly calculating, but it is usually rather frivolous and does not make much headway.

I am going to speak rather personally this evening. I want to read something that might seem strange to read, but again because of Rabbi Schorsch's references I feel comfortable doing so. I want to read the portion of something that moved me passionately into the Jewish–Catholic dialogue from which I have never withdrawn, although I have been shaken very frequently. This is from the concluding portion of that seminal work of Professor Elie Wiesel. He wrote it after he had left the concentration camp, after having seen his mother and two sisters burned in the furnace and with only his father and himself left because they were capable of working. Then his father grew very ill and could no longer work. His father is indeed dying and he describes this particular, horrifying night in their cell block. He said:

> There was silence all around now, broken only by groans. In front of the block, the SS were giving orders. An officer passed by the beds. My father begged me, 'My son, some water. . . . I am burning. . . . My stomach.' 'Quiet, over there!' yelled the officer. 'Eliezer,' went on my father, 'some water. . . .' The officer came up to him and shouted at him to be quiet. But my father did not hear him. He went on calling me. The officer dealt him a violent blow on the head with his truncheon. I did not move. I was afraid. My body was afraid of also receiving a blow. Then my father made a rattling noise and it was my name: 'Eliezer.' I could see that he was still breathing—spasmodically. I did not move. When I got down after roll call, I could see his lips trembling as he murmured something. Bending over him I stayed gazing at him for over an hour engraving into myself the picture of his blood-stained face, his shattered scull. Then I had to go to bed. I climbed into my bunk above my father, who was still alive. It was January 28, 1945. I awoke on January 29 at dawn and in my father's place lay another invalid. They must have taken him away before dawn and carried him to the crematory. He may still have been breathing. There were no prayers at his grave. No candles were lit to his memory. His last word was my name. A summons, to which I did not respond.[4]

---

[4] Elie Wiesel, *Night* (New York: Bantam Books, 1960), pp. 102–103.

That was published in 1960. I did not know Elie Weisel then. However, we have become very close since. So close that I have asked him, indeed publicly on television, "Is it the memory of your failure to respond to your father's call that has haunted you so much throughout your life, that you have relentlessly pursued the Holocaust, determined never to let anyone forget it? So much so that you are often called the voice of Jews from the dead speaking to the living. Is it the echo of your father's voice?" He responded, "Yes, that is what has haunted me."

That is what moved me into the dialogue. I had to ask myself: "Where have you been? Where have you been in the midst of anti-Semitism? Where were you during World War II? Did you ever raise your voice?" Rabbi Lookstein has written a beautiful book on the failure of many Jews to raise their voices. Those Jews were paralleled by the many Catholics who failed to raise their voices.

I spent a portion of today in formal dialogues with a group of rabbis and others and a group of bishops and others. During that dialogue, when we were speaking of the millennium, which is the broad covering title given to this year's symposium on *Nostra Aetate*, I said that I did not know about this; that I could only speculate that the Holy Father would go to Israel in the year 2000; that he would do everything he could to offer midnight mass in Bethlehem, the traditional spot of the birth of Christ; that he would go to Jerusalem to the holy places; again, still speculation on my part, that he would go to Sinai to renew the covenant.

A very learned rabbi said to me "When you are speaking to the Holy Father ask him not to forget Mount Nebo. That, of course, is the mountain on which Moses died, looking into the promised land, which he was prohibited from entering. And as the rabbi said to me, "Mount Nebo is for us a constant reminder that we are not there yet."

We are not there yet in the dialogue between Jews and Catholics. As the Rabbi has said this evening, we have made enormous progress since *Nostra Aetate*, but we are not there yet. We have not achieved that spiritual unity. We have not achieved it because of mistakes in the past. We have not achieved it because of the indifference to which he referred. We have not achieved it because we have not recognized it is our responsibility to achieve it.

This is a wonderful thing that is happening here at Fordham. Like events are occurring all over the United States. I have been involved in others of them. But this is an event that should be taking place in Central Park. This is an event that should be taking place in the largest arena in the United States. Jews and Catholics, Christians and others from all over should recognize its gravity. We should recognize that necessity not only for the public square and for a restoration of moral values in society, as was so well said here this evening, but far beyond that for a fulfillment of the divine promise.

One of the great things done by *Nostra Aetate* was to remind us not that Judaism was, but that Judaism is. It was to remind us that Catholicism is rooted in Judaism. Judaism is our spiritual heritage. Jews are our spiritual ancestors and one does not attempt to destroy one's ancestors. One is proud of one's ancestors. And one lives with one's ancestors as long as they live and as long as you live. Side by side. In peace and in love.

That is what we should be celebrating. That is what the millennium must be about. The millennium must not simply be a celebration of the 2000 years since the birth of Christ, of immense and indispensable importance to Christians. But we should turn to the Jewish community, to the Jewish world, asking: Help us to celebrate this event of such magnitude to both. Help us to celebrate the progress we have made toward spiritual union. Help us to avoid that kind of millenarianism, that kind of Christian triumphalism, that temptation that might occur, to bring about a coalition of the Christians in the world, to shout with triumph against the Jews that we have won. We need the help of the Jewish world to celebrate.

About a year and a half ago the Holy Father called to Rome all the cardinals of the world to discuss explicitly and uniquely preparation for the millennium. One of the dominant themes that developed was that the Church can enter the millennium only if it is attempting to purify itself. The Holy Father himself made the point and he repeats it very, very strongly in his pastoral allocution, in his apostolic letter, "the Coming Third Millennium." He refers to the jubilee. He speaks of the millennium as a jubilee celebration, the term of the Jewish scriptures. The jubilee marked great rejoicing but also great penance. The jubilee was an extraordinary Yom Kippur, a feast, a celebration conjoined with penance, a request for forgiveness and purification.

If we are going to prepare to celebrate *Nostra Aetate* within the context of the millennium, it seems to me that this is an initial requirement: a willingness to be contrite and to be contrite together, whether or not in the balance of history the multiplicity of sins of Christians against Jews is far greater than those of Jews against Christians. This is less germane than the fact that all of us human beings have sinned. All of us have failed to advance the cause of peace with one another, the cause of harmony, the cause of true union. So we all have reason for contrition, for atonement. So it seems to me that first comes this need for repentance. Within this, and, this is myself speaking, it is essential that we all develop a sense of humility.

I happen to have been privileged to have been involved in the dialogue for a number of years, as have Rabbi Schorsch and many others here. But that does not make me an authority. I do not begin to have the answers to the burning questions. Peggy Steinfels put it well: neither of us wants to speak infallibly. There is a little Hasidic tale that frames it well, about a town where it was believed that every Hasidic rabbi could perform miracles. One of the rabbis was a poor man whom nobody took very seriously. But whenever somebody came to him for a miracle he was ready to produce one. One day a woman came to tell him that her husband had gotten lost somewhere and she wanted to know where he was. "Alright, I'll tell you," said the rabbi. He climbed up on a chair and said, "Your husband is 120 kilometers from here. I can see him." When asked whether he could really see that far, the rabbi replied that he could. Then why did you climb on that chair? "I wanted to appear normal," he said.

Secondly, in a spirit of repentance, we must carefully and studiously review the past. We must review it together. We must review what has happened. We must review what we have permitted to happen. In 1963 I was stationed in Monterey, California. I had always thought of myself as a man without prejudice against Jews. No anti-Semitism in my background. I was, therefore, shocked when I was asked to give a talk to a group of Jewish people and at the conclusion, instead of lauding me for my wondrous words, which were gold indeed, they attacked me very forthrightly. They attacked me because of their attitude toward Pope Pius XII. And they were attacking Pope Pius XII because the play, *The Deputy*, had just appeared. *The Deputy* was a formidable attack on Pius XII, and I thought it an unfair attack.

I feel that all of us together must re-examine that period. We have to hope that all of the records will be revealed. We can study them together. But I also discovered that evening that, in a sense more important than the reality of whether Pius XII did or did not do what he should have was the perception that he did not. That is what we are living with today. I remember how *The Deputy* angered many Catholics. It was a great setback for the dialogue. Catholics were angered against Jews. Jews were stirred up against the Pope. Pope Pius XII was virtually an icon for Catholics. Every GI knew Pius XII because during World War II they went to Rome and they saw him. They had never seen a Pope before. It was a terrible setback. But one must learn to deal with perceptions in the dialogue and not be put off by the perceptions.

Nostra Aetate, as has been noted here tonight and on so many occasions since it appeared in October of 1965, was a tremendous boon. Its content was remarkable. But as with so many documents it was so poorly promulgated. There were sixteen major documents at the Second Vatican Council. One could walk through New York for twenty miles, stop the first one and a half million people, and many might tell you all about the spirit of the Second Vatican Council. But if you asked, "Have you ever read a document?" No, they had never read a document of the Second Vatican Council. Some had heard of *Nostra Aetate*. "Have you ever read it?" No, they never read *Nostra Aetate*. One must read it. One must study it. One must see its implications. These are very serious implications.

So many children were brought up to blame the Jews for crucifying Christ. *Nostra Aetate* said that this was not true, this must not be. But it was not until 1974 that the Commission on Religious Relations With the Jews was established and issued guidelines for the execution of *Nostra Aetate*. Among these were very important liturgical guidelines. For years and years on Good Friday we had been praying about the perfidious Jews. These guidelines, as did

Nostra Aetate, demanded that such terminology be dropped. Ultimately, that process has a tremendous impact. It takes many years. Our liturgy was changed. Our catechetical materials were changed. They were scrubbed, not always successfully, nor always fairly. But largely the effort was made to rid them of anti-Semitism. And then came the current catechism of the Catholic Church, which says a great deal further to eliminate anti-Semitism, and weighs very heavily against anti-Semitism. Does it say enough? Some people would think not. Does it say too much? Some would say yes. But here is where humility comes in once again. The catechism is not the end of the world. It does not have the authority of *The New York Times*. But it is a general and comprehensive collection of the beliefs of Catholics. It is very serious about *Nostra Aetate* and anti-Semitism.

Ms. Steinfels was kind enough to refer to my experience at Dachau. And since I said this has to be a personal reflection, I told you it was Elie Wiesel's writings that moved me: about "the Jews of Silence," about the Jews in Russia.

When I came here, I learned that the Archbishop of New York usually goes out to review the parades from the steps of Saint Patrick's Cathedral, all sorts of parades. But I was at lunch one day, after my 10:15 mass, and I heard the sounds of a parade. And I asked someone, "What's that?" I was told it was the Jewish Solidarity parade. "Well, why am I not out there?" "Oh no, the Archbishop never goes out there. That's crazy." But I had read the *The Jews of Silence*. I had read *Night*. So I went out on those steps and I could not believe the impact on the Jews who were marching in that solidarity parade. From that point on, I was with them every year and went over to the United Nations. I gave speeches at the United Nations about the Jews in Russia particularly. It does not make me noble. It is just illustrative of how ignorant and indifferent we can be.

It was not only the writing of Elie Wiesel. It was my own experience in 1974, when I first went to Dachau. I had never been to any concentration camp. I will not detail it—not only because of time but it is too difficult. I weep when I try to. I can tell you only that when I laid my hand on the floor of the semicircular, red brick oven and I felt the intermingled ashes of Jews and Christians and rabbis and ministers and priests and men, I asked myself "Good God, can human beings do this to human beings?" And I determined that I had a responsibility to compensate in some way, to do what I could, somewhere. And on that occasion I felt an almost mystical relationship to Israel. I think I understood for the first time the meaning of the land. The land of the Jews. Not just a piece of dirt. The embodiment of Judaism. The embodiment of Israel. I have written about this in the book I have written with Ed Koch. I have written about this in the book I did with Elie Wiesel. But that just began to burn within me. I then began seizing every opportunity I could to advance the cause of formal diplomatic relations with Israel.

Back in 1904, when the pioneer of Zionism, Theodore Herzl, visited the Cardinal Secretary of State to Pius X (long before Pius XII), Cardinal Merry del Val, and asked for the support of the Holy See for the Zionist movement, the answer he got was this:

> As long as the Jews deny the divinity of Christ, we certainly cannot go along with them. It is not that we despise them at all. On the contrary, the Church has always protected them. For us they are the vital witnesses of what occurred prior to the time when our Lord visited the Earth. Still, they persist in denying the divinity of Christ. How then can we accept the idea that they should regain possession of the Holy Land without disavowing our own highest principles?[5]

In my judgment, that was a gravely mistaken position. I learned, through the dialogue, as many here, that it is absolutely impossible, seriously, to address any issue of substance and interest to Jews and to Catholics for more than, in some instances, thirty seconds and other instances thirty minutes without being confronted with the question, "How can we take the Catholic Church seriously when you refuse to recognize Israel by way of formal diplomatic relations?" There was no answer. I understood the diplomatic reasons: the concern for free access to the holy places in Jerusalem. The concern for the Palestinians in the camps. Anyone who has ever visited them, as I have, shares that concern. Concern for the Christians in the Middle East, who have always been second-class citizens for fear that they would be further persecuted.

---

[5] Entry for January 23, 1904 in *The Diaries of Theodore Herzl* (New York: Universal Library, 1962), p. 421.

I can understand all of that. But I said to myself, the Holy Father is a spiritual entity. The Holy See is a spiritual entity. The power of the Holy See is not in a bureaucracy. It is not in what we call the Roman Curia. It is in the person of the Holy Father. And Israel, the land of Israel, to me, is the embodiment of universal Judaism. Why then cannot there be at least a spiritual diplomatic recognition? I did what I could. On December 30, 1993, the accord was signed. And now it is a new era and a new dialogue. Now we can move to a new approach. For me that approach should be the Bialogue. Not simply talking together but truly living together. Our shared faith. Becoming one people in spirit, while maintaining our religious identities. One in spirit, peace, and love.

Audience member: In addition to the Holocaust, what factors influenced the discussions at Vatican II, and the positive course of Catholic-Jewish relations afterwards? I have in mind, for example, modern biblical scholarship, which led us to read the biblical text in a different light. Also, perhaps, the experience in the United States where Catholics and Jews worked together, for example, in the labor movement?

Ismar Schorsch: My impression is that the American Catholic Church was really in the forefront of the progressive forces at Vatican II and it applied a lot a pressure. There was great resistance. The prelates coming from the Middle East were very concerned about tilting the declaration in favor of the state of Israel and they threw up a lot of resistance. There were conservative forces as well. However, they were overwhelmed and I think that the American experience played a fairly decisive role in creating this new era of Catholic–Jewish dialogue.

Cardinal O'Connor: Yes, I do not think that there is any doubt about the importance of developments in scriptural and theological understanding. One of the speakers here has been Monsignor John Meier, scriptural scholar, who talked about his book, *The Marginal Jew*. It is about Jesus and two volumes are out. It reflects totally new understandings. One of the speakers here was Fr. Ray Brown, who taught at Union Theological Seminary. He has just done a two-volume work on the death of Jesus. There are all sorts of new scriptural understandings.

One, for example, that is now common in our preaching: It used to be the case that we would identify Pharisaism with hypocrisy. Pharisees were the hypocrites of the day. With the new scriptural understanding you come to realize that many Pharisees, a majority of Pharisees, were very respectful and truly kept the law. Only a handful were hypocrites. As for the Scribes, we used to use that word only with contempt, forgetting that they were the lawyers of the day.

The uniqueness of the American experience has been a major contribution. As has been said frequently, there are more Jews in New York City than anywhere in the world. And this is an inescapable and enriching experience for people of all religious persuasions. There have been a lot of sociological advantages. I think an awful lot of anti-Semitism has been successfully attacked. The labor movement that was mentioned is an excellent example of recognition of fighting side by side for justice for all and for the rights of working people and so on.

Audience member: I am very pleased to hear the very beautiful words of Cardinal O'Connor and I would like to address my question to him. The ideas that you expressed are wonderful. Is there any organized attempt, in the Catholic Church, to get these ideas down to the average parishioner in the Church, to the people in the pew?

Cardinal O'Connor: Earlier today in the dialogue that I talked about with rabbis and others on the Jewish side, and bishops and priests on the Catholic side, this very issue was raised and it is so frustrating for all of us. It is true of ninety percent of the documents that come from Rome, unless the papers pick up some portion of them, and often they are taken out of context.

We have our huge system of Catholic schools and we are making the effort. We now have developed a lot of new materials. We have not been satisfied with just cleaning up the old instructional materials. It is probably going to be a long time. I think that the Pope did more in the period of time that he was here than most of us have done in a century, just by his ways, his manner, his way of clearly embracing all peoples. He used a beautiful phrase at the United Nations, which was about the toughest audience anyone can ever speak to—Hindus, Muslims, Buddhists, Jews, Protestants, Catholics—from every part of the world. He asked them to have hope, not to be afraid. That we can all come together so that the tears of this century will water the seeds of a great new life in the next millennium. And I think he touched an enormous number of people. And we have to learn how to do that. We are certainly not anywhere near there yet.

Audience member: I would just like to ask what the two speakers think is the best that young people can do to further the relationships between the Catholic Church, the Jewish people, and other non-Christians. I am the product of sixteen years of Catholic education.

Ismar Schorsch: I want to make a comment about the new catechism. About a year ago when it was just about to appear, I met with Cardinal Law of Boston for an hour and a half. He was very instrumental in the production of the catechism and the supervision of the translation. He gave me a copy, personally inscribed. It is a wonderful book for me to dip into and I have done that on many occasions. It is the first catechism in four hundred years, since the Council of Trent. It is an elegant, comprehensive statement of Catholic belief and practice. It is a document that is readily accessible. I believe it is a document that should be read singly and in community. I could readily imagine that parts of the catechism that deal with Catholic–Jewish relations could be studied together in such dialogue. The catechism does a systematic reinterpretation of New Testament passages that relate to the Jews, especially to the crucifixion. That is the kind of serious material that should be talked through. I believe that much of the spirit of *Nostra Aetate* is captured in the catechism, and that too should be subject to communal reading and dialogue. So I think that the Church has produced an incredible instrument to advance the dialogue between us.

Cardinal O'Connor: I think you can do a lot from a negative perspective, in a sense, personally. It always has to be a personal thing. It cannot be just a document or a movement or a class-room. But just getting disturbed by anti-Semitic jokes—you know that it not an easy thing to do, to tell someone "I do not think that is funny."

There is an Irishman up in the Bronx, I think I read about him in the *Jewish Weekly*, which is a very helpful organ in many re-spects. This fellow came out to his car and discovered vicious, anti-Semitic stickers on his windshield. He also saw them on cars all over that section of the Bronx. He took the trouble to track it down. It made him furious, although he was an Irish Catholic. He discovered that it was one of these groups down South, an offshoot of the American Nazi movement, the same kind of red-neck stuff that Rabbi Heschel discussed regarding the word that could become the deed. Rabin could tell us right now, if he were alive. And you have to get at words from whatever source. That takes courage.

Sometimes when I stand up at the Cathedral I know I am not always talking to people who want to hear what I have to say. I am not necessarily going to win any popularity points when I am talking about anti-Semitism or anti-racism. Once I announced that I was going to give a little bit of money to any black student for scholarship, I got a flood of letters from angry Catholics from a certain section of New York. How dare I give my money, which I did not deserve anyway, to a black student. When I sent a tele-gram to President Reagan, urging him not to go to Bitburg, oh boy did I get ripped to shreds. The largest pile of mail I ever got was sent to me for doing that. But you have to do it. It is the only way.

Audience member: You have both spoken very eloquently for the past thirty years and I am wondering would either of you gentlemen would care to identify one or two areas in which you think Jews and Catholics can work very profitably together for the next thirty years.

Ismar Schorsch: It is a provocative question. One of the things I learned from the Cardinal in one of our previous appearances together was the immensity of the hospital system that the Catho-lic Church runs. It is the largest hospital system in the United

States. I think it is an embodiment of social values of the highest order. Jews also have a hospital system. There are many cities with a Mount Sinai hospital in them. We too have a sense of contribution and social responsibility. We serve not only our own, but the larger community. I think those hospital systems are expressions of compassion for the less fortunate. I think they are a desire to share knowledge and support, especially at this time, when there is such an obsession with balancing budgets that we tend to forget about the weak and the poor. That sense of social responsibility , as manifested in a hospital system, ought to be brought to bear. That is one of the common causes that we ought to jointly pursue.

Another is the school system. We are both concerned with the identity of our young. We labor hard to create a rich, inner life so that our values might be transmitted to the next generation. Mayor Guiliani singled out the parochial school system of the Church here in New York for teaching values. Certainly the day schools of the Jewish community are a similar effort. These are efforts at trying to cultivate a religious identity while remaining deeply committed to the democratic ideal of the open society. So, I think, we have again a lot to contribute to the society as a whole and a lot to learn from each other.

Cardinal O'Connor: I agree with what the Rabbi has to say. I will add very little. Certainly we both have a very strong sense of family values. Clearly, the imbalance and disfunctionality today in the United States in this regard just screams for our mutual assistance, attention, addressing. Not the kind of interference with free speech that the Rabbi was talking about before. But the downright, just incredible, unthinkable pornography that just pours off the television. This could be something that we could address together to the good of all, trying to let the world know that we Jews and Catholics are talking. This is something that would be very helpful and could attract others.

Audience member: I would like to address an important part of the sense of friction, at least in the Jewish community, relating to family values. Cardinal O'Connor, in marriages between Catholics and Jews is it possible for the children of those marriages to be raised as both Jews and Catholics?

Cardinal O'Connor: Earlier today that issue was addressed in the dialogue that I talked about before. Rabbi Mordechai Waxman was, I think, the one who raised it. We agreed in this larger group to appoint a subcommittee to address this. The first step toward it is the preparation of both individuals for marriage. We are getting more and more insistent now that even Catholics marrying Catholics must go through a much more rigorous preparation for it: much more rigorous study of the implications, responsibilities, and the spiritual dimensions of marriage. We have always done this in regard to Catholics marrying Protestants. But only now are both Jewish rabbis and Catholic priests doing this to help prepare Jews to marry Catholics, and vise versa. So we are at the start of the process now, that is, to prepare them.

The next question will be how do they live together? How do they address children? One would have to ask very honestly what does one mean by having them reared jointly as Jewish and Catholic. And there you cannot fudge. There has to be a religious identity. There also must be great understanding of the others. The document that I mentioned from the Commission for Religious Relations With the Jews says that it is an absolute necessity that Catholics come to understand what Jews really teach. What Judaism is all about. What is the history? What is the current practice? And the same is incumbent on Jews. We cannot even talk about being raised in both cultures unless we have a much better understanding of each other than we currently have.

Audience member: I want to ask whether you have any thoughts regarding the problems caused by so-called religious zealots in the Middle East as well as in this country.

Ismar Schorch: An enormous amount of thought. Obviously, what happened in Israel was a national trauma: the assassination of the Prime Minister not by an Arab or a Palestinian, but by a fellow Jew. I think there is a great deal of soul-searching going on in the Jewish community about religious zealotry. I personally think that the lesson to be learned from this tragedy is that you need to read texts carefully. We speak about the consequences of words. There are also consequences to studying sacred texts. I believe very strongly that you cannot take a text and rip it out of its context, and simply apply it to another context that is separated from it by generations and multiple conditions. Texts are products of a specific time and place. And religious zealots have a tendency to rip texts out of context. They also tend to take a tradition which is multivocal, very rich in controversy, and reduce it to a single voice. The Talmud is a nineteen-volume corpus which thrives on dialogue and disagreement and conflict. That is what makes it a fascinating text. To be a student of the Talmud is to enter that eternal dialogue between Israel and God. Between Jew and Jew. That Talmud is a document that does not speak with a single voice. There are many voices to be heard in that Talmud. And to read that Talmud as a single authoritative voice is a dreadful distortion of the corpus and the text.

So, my own passion is to approach those texts with critical scholarship, the kind of scholarship that the Cardinal spoke about a few minutes ago. Religious texts are potent. Read recklessly they can be dangerous. We need to temporize those texts. We need to soften those texts by critical scholarship so that we can come up with the combination of a divine voice and a human voice. None of us is an authority on what God wishes or what is God's will. We seek to hear God's voice to the best of our ability, but what is critical to that quest is a sense of humility, a sense of being fallible, a sense of seeing only part of the picture, of realizing how much is unknown and unfathomable. Therefore, the way, I believe, to temper fundamentalism or zealotry is to make sure that those text are read from the perspective of the twentieth century.

Cardinal O'Connor: A very quick addition from a pragmatic perspective. I have talked in the Middle East to a number of chiefs of state. I will not name them. They have expressed to me their fear about the rise of militancy in various areas in the Middle East, religious militancy. I have a dialogue here, a Catholic–Muslim dialogue. I have a great respect for the Muslims engaging in that dialogue. Many leaders in the Middle East, Muslim leaders, are very much afraid of the militant Islam. Some Arab leaders, some Muslim leaders are very much afraid of Jewish militarism. Everyone out there is afraid of such extremism, and certainly we have to watch for it here.

Jerusalem: Heavenly City and Earthly Center in Jewish and Early Christian Thought

November 14, 1996

Byron Shafer: This evening we are going to be taking a historical approach to the concepts about Jerusalem in Jewish and early Christian thought. We will explore the developments in Jewish and early Christian thinking about Jerusalem as a religious center, developments occurring in the period prior to the Islamic conquest by Caliph Umar around the year 640 of the Common Era.

The Jewish attachment to the earthly city of Jerusalem began over 1600 years before the arrival of Caliph Umar, at the time of the conquest of the Jebusite city of Jerusalem by Israel's King David around the year 993 or so, before the Common Era. David's son and successor, Solomon, was the one who arranged for the construction of the temple which stood in Jerusalem for nearly 400 years until the destruction of Jerusalem and its temple by the Babylonians in the sixth century before the Common Era in 587. At that time most of the population was exiled to Babylon. But in the year 538, the Persian king Cyrus allowed a group of Jews to return to Jerusalem, but without political autonomy.

Twenty years later, under the leadership of the prophets Haggai and Zechariah, the second temple was built in Jerusalem, and Jerusalem and its temple once again became the focus of Jewish faith and religion. The second temple stood for nearly 600 years, during which time Jerusalem was controlled first by the Persians, and then by the Greeks, then briefly by an independent Jewish dynasty known as the Hasmoneans, and then finally by the Romans.

It was in the year 70 of the Common Era that the Romans destroyed Jerusalem and its temple, leveling it to the ground in response to a rebellion which had broken out about four years earlier. In the aftermath of the Roman destruction of Jerusalem in the year 70, the center of active Jewish life and thought in Palestine moved largely to the north, to Galilee. Although the temple has never been rebuilt, the city of Jerusalem has of course remained throughout Jewish history the focus of Jewish hope. Still, given the destruction of Jerusalem and the long absence of a majority Jewish population in the city, Jewish thinkers began, perhaps in the first century of the Common Era, to speak not only of the earthly Jerusalem, Jerusalem below, but also of a heavenly Jerusalem, Jerusalem above.

For first-century Christians, the earthly city of Jerusalem was the site of the death, resurrection, and ascension of Jesus. But among Christians there was greater focus on the concept of a heavenly Jerusalem than attachment to the physical site of Jerusalem. The situation continued until the fourth century, when the Emperor Constantine embraced Christianity and began to build churches throughout Palestine that commemorated the sites of Jesus' life, death, and resurrection. Over the next three centuries, with the building of Christian Palestine, the earthly city of Jerusalem came to be seen by Christians as clothed in heavenly glory.

The topic of this evening's discussion, then, is the developments that took place in Jewish and early Christian understanding of Jerusalem until the time of conquest of Christian Jerusalem by the Persian armies in the year 614 of the Common Era.

Robert L. Wilken: During the past hundred years, and especially since the founding of the state of Israel, the land of the Bible and the land of the Jewish people have been almost inseparable in the consciousness of the West. From the early nineteenth-century Love of Zion societies in eastern Europe to the young Americans who move to new settlements on the West Bank today, the dream of settling the land, of living in the land, of cultivating the land has stirred the minds and hearts of Jews deeply.

The idea of repossessing the land moved Gentiles as well as Jews. George Eliot, who was not a Jew, wrote her most mature novel, *Daniel Deronda*, about a young English orphan who discovered that his natural mother was a Jew. He falls in love with a Jewish woman, Mirah, and under the tutelage of her wise and learned brother, Mordecai Ezra Cohen, Daniel gradually identifies with his people and their hopes. Daniel learns of the ancient dream, revived in the nineteenth century, that one day Jews would return to the land of their fathers and mothers. "Looking towards a land and a polity, our dispersed people in all the ends of the earth may share the dignity of a national life which has a voice among the peoples of East and West. . . ."[1]

Christians, it is thought, have no abiding city. Their hope is set on a heavenly country, on the Jerusalem above, a city not made with human hands. Yet it is evident to any visitor to the Middle East that Christianity has a unique and irreplaceable relation to the lands embraced by the State of Israel, the West Bank, and Jordan. Thousands of Christian pilgrims, borne aloft on the broad wings of Swiss Air and El Al, come from all parts of the world to visit the "holy places" associated with the life of Jesus: Bethlehem, Nazareth, the Church of the Resurrection, the Mount of Olives, the Sea of Galilee and the towns surrounding it. The Christian religion has a long history in Palestine, a history of indigenous communities whose fortunes have been linked to the many con-querors—Romans, Arabs, Crusaders, Turks, and Jews—and of ethnic communities from other parts of the world—Copts from Egypt, Armenians, Syrians, Ethiopians, Russians, et al., some of which have uninterrupted histories from antiquity to the present.

At the end of the fourteenth century a pilgrim from France reported that, on his way from Jerusalem to visit the monastery of St. Catherine in the Sinai, he stayed the night in a village called Beit Jala (two miles from Bethlehem). In this village, he wrote, "we laid in a supply of wine which was delivered by the consul at Jerusalem. Because the Saracens [Muslims] themselves drink no wine, the pilgrims can get it only at very great danger and at a high price." "Beit Jala," he continued, "is populated more by Christians than by Saracens. The Christians work the vineyards where these good wines grow and you may be sure that one can properly call them good wines."[2] To this day Beit Jala remains a Christian village and its inhabitants grow grapes from which they produce wine.

---

[1] George Eliot, *Daniel Deronda* (New York: Oxford University Press, 1984), p. 454.

[2] Roland A. Browne, *The Holy Jerusalem Voyage of Ogier VIII, Seigneur d'Angl-ure* (Gainesville: University of Florida Press, 1975), pp. 41–42.

Christian Jerusalem is at once a fact of history *and* a work of the imagination. The actual city, the place where King David ruled and Jesus of Nazareth was crucified, is irrevocably part of Christian memory. What happened there—whether one thinks of the siege of Nebuchadnezzar in 586 B.C.E., the destruction of the Temple by the Romans in 70 C.E., or the advent of Muslim rule in the seventh century—is no less constitutive of the Christian past than of Jewish history. When the Persians occupied Jerusalem in 614 C.E. it was a Christian monk from Mar Saba, the monastery in the Judean desert east of Bethlehem, who wrote a lament mourning the destruction of the city. What he lamented was not a heavenly city, the new Jerusalem, but the actual city of stone and wood, its marble columns and mosaic floors, its magnificent portals, and of course the temple of God, the holy Anastasis. John the Almsgiver, patriarch of Alexandria, lamented the Persian conquest of Jerusalem not for one day, not for a week, not for a month but for a full year. "Wailing and groaning bitterly, he strove by his lamentations to outdo Jeremiah, who of old lamented the capture of *this same city*, Jerusalem."[3]

But for Christians Jerusalem is also the city of Psalm 87, "Glorious things are spoken of you O city of God," and Isaiah 60, "And nations shall come to your light," a spiritual and theological reality, that came into being with the coming of Christ. When Christians pray the words of Psalm 46, "There is a river whose streams make glad the city of God, the holy habitation of the Most High," they think of the Church, not the city located on the edge of the Judean desert. The spiritual Jerusalem of Christian prayer would, however, never have come into being had wondrous things not taken place in the historical city. Just as it is not possible to tell the Christian story without reference to time, "crucified under Pontius Pilate," in the words of the creed, so one cannot envision Bethlehem without thinking of a place that can be located on a map. When Cleopas and another disciple met Jesus on the road to Emmaus, Cleopas asked Jesus, "Are you the only visitor to Jerusalem who does not know the things that have happened *there*

---

[3] *Life of John the Almsgiver* by Leontius, Bishop of Neapolis, ch. 9. Text edited by Hippolyte Delehaye, "Une Vie inédite de Saint Jean l'Aumonier," in *Analecta Bollandiana* 45 (1927), 23.

in these days?" (Luke 24:18) From the very beginning Christian belief was oriented to events that had taken place in specific city, Jerusalem. Early on, this topographical fact embedded itself deep within the Christian memory, so much so that in the second century a Christian bishop could say that Jesus was crucified "in the middle of Jerusalem."[4] Where Jesus suffered and died and was buried helped impose order on the memory of his life and sowed seeds for the sanctification of space.

Palestine was a Christian country for over three centuries, i.e., from the late fourth century through the Arab conquest in the seventh century and beyond. But Christians have lived there from the beginning of Christianity up to the present time. During the early period, i.e., the fourth to the seventh centuries, the time of Christian hegeomony, Christians began to view the land of the Bible as a Christian Holy Land and Jerusalem as the Christian city par excellence.

The Christian church had its beginnings in the city of Jerusalem. In the book of Acts, the earliest narrative account of Christian beginnings, it is reported that Peter went out into the streets and preached to the "inhabitants of Judea and all who dwell in Jerusalem." From this time there was a Christian community in Jerusalem and the first Christian martyr, Stephen, met his death in the city. In the fourth century a great church was built in Jerusalem outside the Damascus gate to house his relics and honor his memory. The church in Jerusalem was a living link to the events that gave rise to the Christian faith. Only Christians living in Jerusalem could say that these things have been accomplished "among us."

By the second century Christians had begun to visit the "cave" in Bethlehem where Christ was born. Eusebius, the early Christian historian, says that in the third century a certain Alexander from Cappadocia in Asia Minor had gone up to Jerusalem "for the purpose of prayer and seeing the [holy] places."[5] But it was not until the fourth century, after the uncovering of the tomb of Christ in Jerusalem during the reign of the emperor Constantine, that Jerusalem came to be viewed as the holy city by Christians.[6]

---

[4] Melito of Sardis, *Paschal Homily* 94.

[5] Eusebius, *Hist. eccl.* 6.11.2.

[6] For fuller discussion of the Christian identification with Jerusalem and the Holy Land see Robert L. Wilken, *The Land Called Holy. Palestine in Christian Memory and Thought* (New Haven: Yale University Press, 1992).

By the beginning of the fifth century, as the number of pilgrims mounted and people from all over the Christian world became familiar with the geography of Palestine, some discovered that the Holy Land not only had shrines and memorials; it also had a desert—the desert of Elijah, of John the Baptist, and of Jesus. Early in the fifth century Euthymius (known as "the great" to eastern Christians), a monk from Armenia, made the long journey from his native land to settle permanently in the Judean desert. His coming transformed the Judean wilderness into a bustling city, thereby altering the relation of Christianity to the Land of the Bible. Some of the monks took the ancient words to Abraham, "Go up to the land that I will show you" as an injunction to move to Jerusalem. It was these monks who first used the term "holy land" in a self-conscious way to designate the new Christian country. Today Jewish settlements on the West Bank in the Judean desert are built on the same sites that once were inhabited by Christian monks.

During the period extending from the fourth century through the seventh century, the population of Byzantine Palestine had grown rapidly, new buildings were constructed at a dizzying pace, trade increased, the economy flourished, jobs were plentiful (especially for skilled craftsmen and artists), and agriculture and viticulture were extended to previously uncultivated areas, e.g., the Negev and Judean deserts. It is estimated that the number of inhabitants of Jerusalem rose to over fifty thousand from a previous high of ten to fifteen thousand. On the basis of archaeological surveys of the region, it appears that there were four times as many people living in the country in the Christian period than in biblical times. "The Byzantine period . . . indubitably represents a very high point of material development attained by this country," writes the Israeli historian Michael Avi-Yonah.[7] Never before had the size of the population, the volume of trade, the extent of cultivation and usage reached the proportions it did under Byzantine rule.

In the Byzantine period, the inhabitants of the Negev cultivated field crops such as wheat, barley, and various legumes, and grew grapes, olives, dates, and almonds. Byzantine Palestine was, for

---

[7] Michael Avi Yonah, "The Economics of Byzantine Palestine," *Israel Exploration Journal* 8 (1958), p. 40.

Christians, a Holy Land but also a *homeland* a place where men
and women tilled the ground and planted orchards, built homes
and raised families, bought fish and sold olives, buried parents and
grandparents. Many if not most of the churches built in the country were modest, even small, parish churches or monastic chapels
designed to serve the needs of the Christian population of the
land.

These changes did not go unnoticed by the Jews who continued to live in the land. The most tangible evidence of the strength
and vitality of Jewish life during the Christian era in Palestine are
the synagogues excavated in recent years. Best known, of course,
is Bet Alpha in modern-day Beth Shean, but there are many others, in Gush Halav, Nabratein, Rehov, Chorazin, En Gedi, Jeri-
cho, Gaza, and others. The Jews who prayed in these synagogues
could see the changes that were taking place in the land of Israel
as the number of Christians in the land mounted. From scattered
literary references it is clear that these Jews still considered the
land of Israel their land, and looked on the Christians as interlop-
ers. Yet they sensed that these Romans were different from the
Romans who proceeded them. For unlike the pagan Romans for
whom Jerusalem was a foreign city on the edge of the Roman
Empire, these new Romans had designs on the city. With the
Christians something new was added. As a medieval Jewish writer
put it: "The Romans who destroyed the Temple in the days of
the wicked Titus . . . made no claim that they had an inheritance
in the Holy Temple or that it was a fit place of prayer for them.
But when the wicked Constantine was converted they made
these claims."[8]

The most illuminating period in the history of Christianity's
relation to Jerusalem occurs in the seventh century at the time of
the Persian and Muslim conquests. Nothing exemplifies better the
transformation that had taken place over the course of six centuries than the obvious yet seldom observed fact that when Jerusalem was captured by the Persians in the seventh century of the
Common Era, it was the Christians, not the Jews, who sang a
lamentation over the Holy City. We are fortunate to have a Chris-

---

[8] Text from Abraham Bar Hiyya, in *Sefer Megillat ha Megalleh*, ed. Z. Boznanski
(Berlin: 1924).

tian "lamentation" written at the time of the conquest by a monk from Mar Saba.[9] This treatise describes the occupation of the city and the fate of the patriarch of Jerusalem, Zacharias, who was taken into captivity by the Persians.

The most arresting passage in the book occurs at the place where the author is describing the sack of the city by the Persians, using Biblical language to depict the pillaging of holy things and the killing of women, children, and priests. He wrote: "And the Jerusalem above wept over the Jerusalem below." This sentence would have been inconceivable on the lips of a Christian author in earlier centuries. I need only remind you of the words of Melito of Sardis in his paschal homily written in the second century: "The Jerusalem below was precious, but it is worthless now because of the Jerusalem above."[10] Christians had learned to love the Jerusalem below; God did have a dwelling place on earth, and it was the same city in which the glory of the Lord had once dwelt: Jerusalem.

Christian attachment to Jerusalem is evident in another dramatic passage in the book, the account of Zacharias, the patriarch being led out of the city in chains to be taken in captivity to Persia.[11] As Zacharias was led from the city, the people followed him down into the Kidron valley and up the Mount of Olives, where the band of captives halted briefly. At this point "they raised their eyes and beheld Jerusalem ablaze with flames and began to lament." Zacharias turned for one last look at "Zion" and cried out: "O Zion, with a sorrowful word that makes one weep I speak peace to you; peace be with you O Jerusalem, peace be with you O *Holy Land*, peace on the whole land. . . . O Zion, what hope do I have, how many years before I will see you again? What use is there for me, an old man, to hope? . . . I will not see your face again. . . . O Zion, do not forget me your servant, and may your creator not forget you. For if I forget you, O Jerusalem,

---

[9] Text is available only in Arabic and Georgian versions. For a partial English translation of the Georgian text see Frederick C. Conybeare, "Antiochus Strategos' Account of the Sack of Jerusalem in A.D. 614," *The English Historical Review* 25 (1910), pp. 502–516. For discussion with citations translated into English see *The Land Called Holy*, chs. 11 and 12.

[10] Melito is drawing on the words of St. Paul in Galatians 4:26.

[11] For fuller discussion with references see *The Land Called Holy*, pp. 218ff.

let my right hand wither. Let my tongue cleave to the roof of my mouth if I do not remember you. Peace on you, O Zion, you who were my city, and now I am made a stranger to you. . . . To die and to be run through with a sword is sweeter than to be separated from you, O Zion."

When Zacharias saw the people throwing ashes over their heads and beating their breasts, he raised his hand to calm them. Then he opened his mouth and spoke to them for the last time. He turned toward Zion, and as a husband consoles his wife, so Zacharias comforted Zion. He extended his hands as he wept, saying: "O Zion, with a sorrowful word that makes one weep I speak peace to you; peace be with you O Jerusalem, peace be with you O Holy Land, peace on the whole land. . . O Zion what hope do I have, how many years before I will see you again. . . . O Zion do not forget me . . . and may your creator not forget you."

This extraordinary scene reminds one of David's departure from the city after the revolt of Abasalom, recorded in 2 Samuel 15. As David left the city, crossed the brook Kidron, and ascended the Mount of Olives he was followed by the people of the city. As he went up the ascent of the Mount of Olives, "weeping as he went, barefoot and with his head covered, all the people who were with him covered their heads and they went up weeping as they went."

Although the Christians were able to drive out the Persians and restore Christian rule in the city in 629 C.E., within less than a decade a new and unknown foe appeared out of the deserts of Arabia. Unlike the Persian occupation of Jerusalem, Islam's conquest of Christian Palestine (634–38 C.E.) was not a temporary scourge that would soon pass. With the arrival of Muhammad's armies and the swift establishment of Arab hegemony in the region, Christian rule in Jerusalem came to an end, decisively and definitively. The commanders of the Muslim armies were disciples and heralds of a new civilization.

The arrival of the Muslims did not, however, spell the end of Christian life in the Holy Land. Most of the Christians in Palestine were indigenous to the region and their lives went on undisturbed, at least initially. Ten years ago, in the summer of 1986, a team of Italian archaeologists excavated several Christian churches in Jordan at Um er-Rasas, a site not far from Madaba (where the sixth century map of the Holy Land had been found). Set in the floor of one of the churches were panels depicting cities in Palestine, Jordan, and Egypt: Jerusalem, called the "Holy City," Neapolis (Nablus), Sebastia, Caesarea, Diosopolis (Lod), Eleutheropolis (Beth-Guvrin), Ascalon, Gaza, Philadelphia (Amaan), Madaba, Alexandria, and others. The church includes two dated mosaics, one dedicated in 756 C.E., a second dedicated in 785 C.E.

In the early eighth century the Muslim Caliph Al-Walid called Syria (which included Palestine) the "country of the Christians" where one could find "beautiful churches whose adornments were a temptation and whose fame was widespread, as for example, the church of the Resurrection and the churches of Lod (Lydda) and Edessa; he therefore undertook to construct for the Muslims a mosque [in Damascus] which would attract them away from these churches, and he made it one of the wonders of the world."[12]

It is apparent that Christianity was not a passing phenomenon in the history of the Holy Land. Accordingly, it is of some historical interest that in Palestine Christians first began to adopt Arabic, the language of the conquerors, as a language for Christian worship and scholarship.

For Christians Jerusalem and the Holy Land are not simply a fascinating chapter in the Christian past. As Jerome wrote to his friend Paula in Rome urging her to come and live in the Holy Land, "The whole mystery of our faith is *native* to this province and city."[13] Nothing else in Christian experience can make this claim; nothing has such fixity. No matter how many centuries have passed, no matter where the Christian religion has set down roots, Christians remain wedded to the land that gave birth to Christ and the Christian religion.

Land, alas, is immovable; like mountains and seas it is stationary. If it should happen that the only Christians to survive in the Holy Land were caretakers of the holy places, Christianity would forfeit a precious part of its inheritance. Like Judaism and Islam, Chris-

---

[12] See *The Land Called Holy*, pp. 247–54.
[13] Jerome, Epistle 46.3.

tianity is not a European religion. Its homeland is in the Middle East, and continuity with its past is dependent on the Christians who continue to live in that land in which the faith is native. Were the holy places turned into museums or archaeological curiosities, as they have been in Turkey or Tunisia, the tangible links that stretch back through history to the apostles and to God's revelation in Christ would be severed. Without the presence of living Christian communities, the witness of the Holy Land can only be equivocal. The martyrs and teachers, the monks and bishops, the faithful who lived in Bethlehem or Beit Jala or Nazareth or Jerusalem, would no longer be signs of a living faith, but forgotten names from a distant past. Bethlehem would become a shrine and Christian Jerusalem a city of ancient renown. Only people, not stones and earth and marble, can bear an authentic witness.

THE EARTHLY AND HEAVENLY JERUSALEM IN CLASSICAL JUDAISM

Michael Fishbane: The *Nostra Aetate* dialogue this year provides a welcome opportunity to discuss the centrality of Jerusalem in Jewish and Christian religious thought during the early centuries of our era. This was a period of classical consolidation, with great influence upon later theology and belief. For my part, I would like to consider images of the earthly and the heavenly Jerusalem in early Jewish literature. In doing so I shall pay particular attention to the phenomenon of sacred space and its place in collective memory and expectation.

Now to speak of sacred space, as any historian of religion knows, is not to speak of a vague or neutral sphere, but one marked by exceptional and transformative qualities. This is something we all know to some degree from personal experience. Who cannot attest to the place special spaces have on our own sense of self and our recollection of events of personal significance? Years ago, the great French phenomenologist Gaston Bachelard wrote a powerful book entitled *The Poetics of Space* (New York: Orion Press, 1964), in which he showed how the spaces we inhabited in our childhood are part of our deepest consciousness and saturated with still-palpable odors and sensations.

What is more, the nooks and crannies of this place remain a primary template for our mature imagination and for our ongoing sense of space and its habitation.

Exceptional locations have an equally significant role in our cultural lives. Think of how Abraham's journey to Canaan, or Moses' experience at the burning bush, or David's actions at the threshing floor of Araunah the Jebusite had irreversible implications for their descendents. Each of the spaces is different and represents a different concern, but together they are foundational moments for the notion of a sacred homeland, the revelation of a divine covenant, and the establishment of a House of God on earth. As members of religious cultures we receive and recite the narratives of these moments and embed them in the archeology of our cultural memory. In this way they become part of our own biographies and sense of space.

A further aspect about sacred space may be mentioned at this point, and that is that each locus has concrete particularity—it is here, not there, where this occurred and not that. I would even stress that precisely because each special place is unique, diverse symbols and narratives, and in time new experiences, are drawn to it. The result is that the specific place is transformed into a symbolic locus comprised of diverse layers of tradition. An Israelite pilgrim would thus come to Zion with different sensibilities and notions in mind than a Jew from Alexandria coming to the Herodian Temple in Jerusalem during Roman times. And further, when an original community with shared narratives splits over theological or other matters, the same site may become important for altogether new and even contentious reasons.

The emerging history of Jerusalem is a case in point. Its role for the ancient Pharisee was altogether different from that of the Qumran sectarian, who believed that the city was utterly defiled by the ruling priesthood and leadership, and should not be entered during this era of history. Similarly, with the growth of Christianity and Islam, the older shared narratives of the Hebrew Bible and early Jewish tradition were supplemented by other narratives deemed to exceed it in value and authority. Multiple images of Jerusalem developed, with contesting claims and different roles in the drama of history and salvation.

All this may be obvious, but I dare say that it bears repetition if only because we tend to forget just how complex the religious imagination is, and just how layered are the images that shape our consciousness. Ecumenical discourse must begin with this point, if ever we may hope to appreciate how diverse communities of faith are constituted. The following discussion hopes to contribute to that dialogue by surveying some of the dominant ideas of Jerusalem held by Jews in late antiquity.

I

In this spirit, I turn to the subject at hand and invoke its ancestral preconfigurations in ancient Israel. I do so for programmatic and principled reasons. Any discussion of Jewish conceptions of Jerusalem (or most any topic) must begin with the Hebrew Bible, the foundation document of the culture, of undisputed authority and centrality. As such, this text has been studied and interpreted for over two and one-half millenia. Indeed, by the time of the redaction of the Babylonian Talmud in the fifth to sixth centuries C.E., the Hebrew Bible had already been the object of intense investigation for one thousand years. By this means, the language and imagery of Scripture entered the cultural imagination of Jews and Judaism. Changes in the role and status of Jerusalem was part of this larger process. It therefore behooves us to review some key features of the subject found first in the literature of ancient Israel and then in new and transformed ways in classical Judaism.

Jerusalem was not originally a sacred city, but a Canaanite one that took on holy features for the Israelites through the transfer to it of the Ark of the Covenant during the reign of David, and subsequently through the building of a Temple there by his son Solomon. The sphere marked off as sacred due to the presence of the Shrine thus became a permanent and constitutive feature of the area. These events were celebrated in liturgical song, and nowhere more authoritatively than in Psalm 132, where we read:

> For the Lord has chosen Zion,
>   He has desired it for His own dwelling, [and said]:
> "This is My resting-place for all time;
>   Here I shall dwell, for I desire it.
> I shall surely bless its store of food,
>   and sate its needy with bread.

> I shall clothe its priests with victory,
>   and its faithful ones shall shout for joy.
> There I shall make a horn sprout for David;
>   I have prepared a lamp for My annointed one.
> I shall cover his enemies with disgrace,
>   but his crown shall gleam upon him" (vv. 13–18).

The effect of divine habitation in Zion thus radiates outward as beneficence for all. Particularly important is the combination of blessings for the priests and monarchs. Jerusalem is thus neither a cultic site nor royal city alone, but both, and God's dwelling there benefits both institutions and the people as well.

People living outside the confines of the city oriented their cultic and spiritual life toward it through pilgrimage. Coming to this place they could hope to partake of its two benefits: holy blessing from the House of the Lord and justice from the king and his courts. There are many psalms that give expression to one or another of these two benefits. Psalm 122 is especially striking insofar as it emphasizes both features, and also preserves something of the human tone of enthusiasm and expectation that marked a visit to God's city of Zion.

> I rejoiced when they said to me,
>   "Let us go to the House of the Lord."
> Our feet stood inside your gates, O Jerusalem,
>   Jerusalem built up, a city joined together,
>   to which the tribes made pilgrimage,
>   the tribes of the Lord,—
>   as was enjoined upon Israel—
>   to praise the name of the Lord.
> There the thrones of judgment stood,
>   thrones of the house of David.
> Pray for the well-being of Jerusalem;
>   "May those who love you be at peace.
> May there be well-being within your ramparts,
>   Peace in your citadels."
> For the sake of my kinsmen and friends,
>   I pray for your well-being;
>   for the sake of the House of the Lord our God,
>   I seek your good.

For the pilgrim, Jerusalem is a place of longing and celebration, where the Lord might be praised and justice established. It is, moreover, a beloved place that is itself the object of prayer—for the sake of the House of the Lord, and for all who depend upon heavenly blessings.

But even as Zion is a space to which all might come, the pilgrim should be a person of rectitude and piety. The prophet Isaiah therefore denounced those who committed sins and came into the Shrine with outstretched hands, hoping to expiate their crimes through sacrifices and entreaty (Isaiah 1:10–17). Others hoped to restrict such incursions through a declaration of the moral and spiritual qualities to be cultivated by those who sought nearness to God in His House. Psalm 15 has been called a liturgy of entrance for that reason. It opens with a question (by the pilgrim): "Lord, Who may sojourn in Your tent, who may dwell on Your holy mountain?" The extensive answer (provided by the guardians of the gates) states that only those who are blameless within and without, whose heart and actions are pure, and who honor those who fear the Lord and never take advantage of their neighbor, may merit this honor. A similar query and answer is found in Psalm 24:3–6, in more condensed form. Clearly, such strict requirements would have limited access to the Temple to a very few, and would have prevented sinners from performing rites of expiation. Accordingly, we may assume that these lists were less an enforceable code than a catalogue of ethical and spiritual ideals. They reflect the sensibility that God's House was a holy space in which only the pure and godfearing were worthy of entrance.

In a more visionary mode, Isaiah also evokes the atmosphere of a pilgrimage when he prophecies a time when all nations will come to the House of the Lord in Jerusalem for justice and instruction. For him, in fact, Zion will become a new Sinai, a place of divine revelation for all. Its glorious effect will be universal peace.

> In the days to come,
> The mountain of the Lord's House
> Shall stand firm above the mountains . . .
> And the many peoples shall go and say:
> "Come, Let us go up the Mount of the Lord,
> To the House of the God of Jacob;
> That He may teach us of His ways,

And we shall walk in His paths."
For Torah [instruction] shall come forth from Zion,
The word of the Lord from Jerusalem.
And He will judge among the nations
And arbitrate for many peoples,
And they shall beat their swords into plowshares
And their spears into pruning hooks:
Nation shall not take up sword against nation,
Or learn the skills of war, anymore (Isaiah 2:2–4).

In the post-exilic period, the images of Zion/Jerusalem un-
dergo a decisive change. Two interrelated topics are of immediate
interest. The first is the polarity of mourning/joy; the other is the
personification of Zion as a woman. This connection emerges
with the lamentations expressing the destruction of the first Temple (587\6 B.C.E.). The "city" sits "lonely . . . like a widow;"
"She weeps bitterly in the night, her cheek wet with tears, there
is none to comfort her" (Lamentations 1:1–2). The dominant epi-
thet used for this figure is *bat tziyon*, literally "daughter of Zion,"
but often rendered as "Fair Zion." She functions as a mystic embodiment of the city and nation. Her citizens are "infants . . .
gone into captivity" (1:5–6); her "uncleanliness . . . clings to her
skirts" (v. 9). "The Lord in His wrath has shamed Fair Zion";
"mourning and moaning" were "increased within [her]" (2:1, 5).
Even the remaining ramparts are invoked to mourn. "O wall of
Fair Zion, shed tears like a torrent day and night. . . . Arise, cry
out into the night at the beginning of your watches, pour out
your heart like water before the Lord. Raise your hands to Him
for the life of your infants, who faint for hunger on every street"
(2:18–19).

The desolation of Zion dominated the consciousness of the exiles in Babylon, and they swore never to forget Jerusalem, no
matter what the circumstances. "If I forget you [*eshkakhekh*], O
Jerusalem, may my right hand forget its cunning; may my tongue
cleave to the roof of my mouth if I do not remember you—if I
do not set Jerusalem above my chiefest joy" (Psalm 137:5). The
"mourners of Zion" determined to keep the mind filled with
memories, out of sorrow, loyalty and hope. Others fell into de-
spair, as we can hear from a lament put into the mouth of Zion.
Echoing the cry of the ramparts in the Book of Lamentations, and

counterpointing the oath just cited, the city cries that "The Lord has forsaken me, My Lord has forgotten me [*shekhekhani*]" (Isaiah 49:14). But now God answers, providing comfort to her sorrow with His own vow: "Can a woman forget her baby or disown the child of her womb? Though she might forget, I could never forget you [*eshkakhekh*]. See, I have engraved you on the palm of My hands, your walls are ever before Me" (vv. 15–16). The "children" will soon return, declares God, who also promises that "You shall deck yourself with them like a bride . . . [and] your ruins and desolate places . . . shall soon be crowded with settlers. . . . And you will say to yourself, 'Who bore these for me when I was mourning and barren. . . . I was left alone, and where have these been?!' " (49:19–21).

Indeed, in another image, the "barren one" is told to shout for joy, for God will espouse her anew as mother and bride (Isaiah 54; 62:4–5). Earthly Jerusalem shall be wondrously consoled. She shall arise in glory, and all nations shall flow to her light (Isaiah 52:1; 60:1–7). All shall call her "City of the Lord, Zion of the Holy One of Israel" (60:14). Now the lamenting towers shall be dried of tears, as God will set watchmen upon the walls of Jerusalem who shall never be silent, day or night, until the Lord Himself "establish Jerusalem and make her renowned throughout the earth" 62:6–7). Echoing this joy, a psalmist exults that the Lord "loves the gates of Zion . . . more than all the dwellings of Jacob" (87:2). "Glorious things are spoken of you, O city of God. . . . Indeed, it shall be said of Zion, 'Every man was born there' (vv. 3, 5). Translating the last verse, the Greek Septuagint rendered Zion as *mater sion*, "mother Zion"—a metropolis for all, a mother of all nations. The national hope has been universalized.

One further feature marks post-exilic depictions of Jerusalem, and show a transformed consciousness of its status. That change is the new depiction of Jerusalem as a "sacred city" (*'ir qodesh*) (Isaiah 48:2; cf. 52:1 and Daniel 9:24). The city thus attains something of the sanctity of place that belongs to the Temple. A related characterization is articulated by the prophet Zechariah, who spoke of Jerusalem as *'admat qodesh*, or "sacred land" (Zechariah 2:14–16). In this way the city becomes a sacred site—a feature of marked importance in early rabbinic thought, as we shall see.

II

With these considerations in mind, we may now turn to the treatment of Zion and Jerusalem in ancient Judaism during the first four centuries of the common era. During this time old time biblical religion was fully transformed into Judaism, and the older images of Scripture were fundamentally reinterpreted by the believing community.

Dominating the reality of this period are expressions of loss at the destruction of the second Temple (70 C.E.) and the Roman regulations preventing access to the city. Assertions of hope stand overagainst this condition. Groups of mourners developed ascetic rites as an expression of their grief, and more moderate rabbinic authorities were pressed to develop less extreme rituals of remembrance. Thus those who build new homes left a portion unplastered "in memory of Jerusalem" [zekher li-Yerushalayim], even as portions of meals were kept set aside and jewelry left unfinished for the same reason (Tosefta Sota 15:10–15). Not forgetting the earthly city was thus but one aspect of the matter; the other was the positive act of remembrance.

Other expressions of ritualized recollection found their way into the liturgy. Hope in the future was always couched in the language of present sorrow. Quite typical is the invocation that God "Make us rejoice at the consolation of Zion, Your city, and at the building of Jerusalem, Your holy city"—recited as part of the grace after every meal. The longing for restoration and redemption is further articulated in Amida-prayer recited thrice daily, in the words: "Return in compassion [O Lord] to Jerusalem, Your city, and dwell in it as You have said; and build it soon in our day as an everlasting structure; and swiftly establish the throne of David within it." And if this were not enough, God is ever reminded to "Have compassion on Zion, for she is the house of our life" in the concluding blessings to the reading from the prophets on Sabbaths and festivals. In these (and many other) forms Jerusalem is placed at the center of human religious consciousness—in fulfillment of an ancient vow of remembrance.

Particularly striking in this regard is the addition to the Amida recited on the Ninth of Ab, the day wholly given over to mourning for Zion. "Comfort, O Lord our God, . . . the city that is in mourning, laid waste, despised and desolate: in mourning—for she is childless; laid waste—in her dwellings; despised—on the downfall of her glory; and desolate—through the loss of her inhabitants. She sits like a barren woman who has not given birth." One will particularly note the midrashic or exegetical character of this version of the prayer (a feature not uncommon in classical prayers), and the emphasis on the trope of the female. Thus a triad of terms dealing with the present desolation of Zion are glossed with reference to mother Zion's mourning over her lack of children. Comfort is beseeched by those who yet remember.

In the earlier Midrash the same trope notably occurs in a homily which describes how the prophet Jeremiah meets a woman in mourning for her husband "who went far away from her," and for her seven sons who, in their father's absence, were killed when a house fell upon them. Jeremiah seeks to console the woman by telling her that "You are not better than my mother Zion, and yet she became pasture for the beasts of the field." But she responds: "I am your mother Zion; I am the mother who lost her seven children" (*Pesikta Rabbati*, 26; Friedmann, ed. 131b). A strikingly similar tradition occurs earlier in 4 Ezra 9:38, 10:1–54, where now the sorrowing woman is seen by Ezra, and this event and the vision of an established city is explained by the angel Uriel as Zion's desolation and restoration.

Visions of a new Jerusalem supplement depictions of its desolation. Two poles are dominant. One is an account of the apocalyptic manifestation of a heavenly Jerusalem on earth. This recurs in pseudepigraphic sources of the early centuries. Typical is Enoch's vision of "a new House, greater and loftier than the first one, and set up in the first location . . .—all its pillars were new, the columns new, and the ornaments new as well as greater than those of the first" (1 Enoch 90:26). Or in another form, the Lord tells Baruch that the new Jerusalem is not the present desolate site, but "the city of which I said 'On the palms of My hands I have carved you' " [Isaiah 49:16, citing the Peshitta version]. This heavenly city was "prepared from the moment I decided to create Paradise"; It was shown to Adam, Abraham, and Moses in the past and "will be revealed" on earth in the future to come (2 Baruch 4:2). For the present, "the highest Jerusalem" is in "the highest heaven" (2 Enoch 55:2).

The idea of a heavenly Jerusalem formed by God before the creation is also known in rabbinic tradition (*b. Pesahim* 54a). But what is intriguing is not only the uniqueness of this tradition in recorded sources, but also the paucity of references to a heavenly Jerusalem altogether. In the one early reference, Rabbi Yohanan ascribed to God's statement in Hosea 11:9 an altogether unexpected meaning. According to the biblical text, it would appear that God stresses that since He is "The Holy One in your midst [*be-qirbekha qadosh*], [therefore] I shall not come in fury [*ba-'ir*]" to mean that "I shall not enter the heavenly Jerusalem until I enter the earthly Jerusalem." The sage has utterly transformed its sense, presumably construing the passage as suggesting that because "the Sanctuary [*qadosh*] is in your midst [*be-qirbekha*]," Jerusalem, "I shall not not come into the [heavenly] city [*ba-'ir*] [before entering the earthly one]" (*b. Taanit* 5a). The transformative nature of this exegesis suggests that a polemical point motivates it. Perhaps the reason for this is explained by another statement attributed to Rabbi Yohanan, in which we are told that "the heavenly Jerusalem is set overagainst the earthly one;" and that "because of His great love for the [Jerusalem] on earth [God] made another in heaven, as it is said, "See, I have engraved you [Jerusalem] on the palms of My hands, your walls are ever before me" [Isaiah 49:16] (*Midrash Tanhuma, Pequdei*, 1). This shift from engraving an image of Jerusalem on the hands as a divine memorial to creating a heavenly replica out of love directly contradicts the idea of a primordial Jerusalem, and would seem to point to a deliberate stress on the primacy in time and quality of the earthly Jerusalem. Some hint of old controversies regarding the future Temple are probably involved.

The centering of religious hopes on the city of Jerusalem below also explains the increasing emphasis on the sanctity of Jerusalem and its environs in early sources. We observed earlier that the prophet Zechariah provides an ancient witness to this development. Later texts provide a more rhetorical rationale for the hierarchization of space. Among these, two have had immense influence on Jewish thought and belief over the ages. The first comes from the Midrash *Mekhilta de-Rabbi Ishmael* (*Bo*, 1), and states:

Before the land of Israel had been especially chosen, all lands were suitable for divine revelation; after the land of Israel had been chosen, all other lands were eliminated. Before Jerusalem had been especially selected, the entire land of Israel was suitable for altars; after Jerusalem had been selected, all the rest of the land of Israel was eliminated. For thus it is said: "Take heed that you do not offer your burnt offerings in every place that you see, but [only] in the place which the Lord shall choose" (Deuteronomy 12:13–14). Before the Temple had been especially selected, the whole of Jerusalem was appropriate for the manifestation of the Divine Presence (the *Shekhinah*); after the Temple had been selected, the rest of Jerusalem was eliminated. For thus it is said: "For the Lord has selected Zion, He has desired it for His habitation: This is My resting place forever" (Psalm 132:13–14).

As is clear, this teaching provides a concise history of sacred space in ancient Israel—but it does so in a hierarchical manner peculiar to rabbinic discourse. It attests to an ever-contracting account of the land which the holy *Shekhinah* could inhabit, beginning with the whole world but ending up with the Temple area alone. There is both a drama of restriction and a focusing of the sacred. The effect is the neutralization of all other spaces— including the Land of Israel—from supreme importance. Quite otherwise is the following extract from *Mishnah Kelim* (I.6–9), where we see a progressive focusing on the holy areas of Jerusalem, but without eliminating the (lesser) sanctity of other areas. In this source, which betrays a strong priestly quality, even the whole of the Land has a sacred quality. This is as unexpected from earlier sources as it proved significant for later halakha and belief. The pertinent section of the Mishnah teaches as follows:

There are ten [ascending] degrees of [spatial] holiness.

1. The Land of Israel is holier than all [other] lands. And in what does its [special] holiness consist? In that people bring [to the Temple] from it [on the Feast of Weeks, the offerings of] the *omer*, the first-fruits, and the two [loaves] of bread—[gifts] which are not brought from any [other] land.
2. Walled cities [in the Land of Israel] are holier than it [the whole of the Land], for lepers are banished from within them, and people may carry a corpse within them as long as they like, but once it has left [the city] they may not bring it back.

3. [The area] inside the wall [of Jerusalem] is holier than they [the other walled cities], for people eat there [the] Lesser Holy Offerings and [the] Second Tithe.
4. The Temple Mount is holier than it [Jerusalem], for men and women with fluxes, menstruant woman, and women who have just given birth, may not enter there.
5. The rampart [of the Temple courts] is holier than it [the Mount], for gentiles and those defiled by a corpse may not enter there.
6. The court of [Israelite] women is holier than it [the rampart], for those persons impure for a day may not enter it, though they are not liable for a sin-offering [if they enter inadvertently].
7. The court of [Israelite] men is holier than it [the women's court], for those without atonement [offerings, for their purification] may not enter there, and are liable for a sin-offering [if they enter inadvertently].
8. The court of priests is holier than it [the men's court], for Israelites may not enter there except to lay hands [on an offering], slaughter, and wave [the cereal-offering].
9. [The area] between the porch and the altar is holier than it [the priestly court], for those [priests] who are blemished and whose hair falls loose may not enter there.
10. The sanctuary is holier than it [the area between porch and altar], for only those who have sashed their hands and feet may enter there.
11. The Holy of Holies is holier than it [the sanctuary], for only the high priest on the Day of Atonement at the time of the [rite of] atonement may enter there.

The account of the heavenly and earthly Jerusalem in early Judaism could be further extended were one to develop any of the themes and types suggested above. Sufficient and representative examples have nevertheless been given to suggest the complex symbolic matrices that constituted the ideas of Zion and Jerusalem in Jewish antiquity. It is important to bring these matters to mind, as I suggested earlier, precisely because of the dominating power these images have had in Jewish consciousness, hope, and belief. It is also important to observe how the multiple images of biblical literature combine or diverge to assume symbolic significance. The Jewish religious imagination is a composite of them all.

Looking back over the whole, we may return to our opening observations that sacred space is always particular, and that with the diversification of belief and practice the same sacred space may be filled with new and competing claims. What the old Essene community means by its vision of the expansion and fulfillment of Isaiah 54:11–12 (in 4 QpIsa[d] = 4Q164) is different from what is found in Jewish sources (*Pesiqta de-Rav Kahana* 20.7) or in the apocalyptic vision in early Christianity (Revelation 21:23, 14, 19–20). This led to conflict and contestation in antiquity. Matters only got worse in the Middle Ages; and the effect of competing claims to Jerusalem is also a fact of our own political times. Old images fuel ongoing passions, and communal interpretations bind the faithful into ever narrower and more exclusionary units. The religious believer of the modern age must therefore decide whether to perpetuate this difficulty or try to overcome it.

In the ecumenical spirit of our gathering, I would offer two models for consideration. They are based on two textual images. One is found in the Hebrew Bible, the other in ancient rabbinic sources. The biblical model is based on the words of the prophet Micah, who cites and reinterprets the aforenoted words of Isaiah. That prophet spoke of a future time when all nations would ascend to Jerusalem and come to the House of the Lord. Micah adds one significant detail. After reciting Isaiah's prophecy of the new Sinai at Jerusalem, and his vision of universal peace, he says: "Though all the people shall walk each in the names of its god, we shall walk in the name of the Lord our God forever and ever" (Micah 4:6). Here is a universal vision that does not assume the conversion or assimilation of peoples to only one religious way. Rather, the prophet suggests that the different peoples shall retain their traditions and gods, their ways and practices, and be united in their common focus on justice and right. Over against Isaiah's formulation, Micah proffers an image of an international federalism, a vision of difference within unity in Jerusalem.

The second model comes from rabbinic tradition. Commenting on the miracles that took place within Jerusalem during the days of the Temple, one teaching has it that when all the populace gathered in the courts "they stood packed in together, but bowed down [in worship] with much room to spare." That is, while there appeared to be little room for personal expression, when the people prayed they were able to do so without hindrance and without infringing upon the space of their neighbor. The image thus transforms a crowded public sphere into a place in which the needs of each worshipper can be met—when their focus is on holiness and celebration.

Like the biblical word from Micah, this rabbinic text offers a challenge to our moral and religious consciousness. It is my hope that they may collectively suggest terms for an ecumenical dialogue to come. Our need for sacred and particular space has not diminished; neither has the necessity for a shared world.

Byron Shafer: Robert and Michael, during the fourth through the seventh centuries when Christian influence was increasing so dramatically in Palestine, did the Jewish and Christian communities exist as separate communities, keeping each other at arm's length, or was there any kind of contact or dialogue between and among these communities?

Robert Wilken: There was certainly much contact, and there was some dialogue. The archeological evidence that we have shows, for example, that a place such as Beth Shean, which in antiquity was named Scythopolis, was a city that included Jews and Christians and others. That would be the case in several of the more Hellenized cities within ancient Roman Palestine.

The evidence for dialogue between Christians and Jews comes primarily from the Christian side. For reasons that scholars cannot explain, we do not know why Jewish literature does not respond to Christianity during the whole period of Christian growth. There are some references, but in the main the character of the literature is such that the matter does not come up. If you read, however, the commentaries of Jerome on the Hebrew Prophets, it is clear that he had much assistance from Jews in his work on the Hebrew texts of the Bible. He was translating into Latin for the first time, and he had that contact through Jewish scholars who were living in the land.

Furthermore, when he comes to passages that speak about the restoration of Jerusalem, he says that the Jews understood these passages, and he uses the Latin phrase *carnaliter*, "in a fleshly sense." It really means "in a political sense." That is, they still hoped that the city of Jerusalem would be restored as the capital of a Jewish kingdom. So there is significant evidence from writings of that sort of Jewish–Christian contact, and there are also isolated references: a stray phrase in an Aramaic targum or a text here or a text there, where you can see that Jews are beginning to realize how different the Christian Romans are from the previous Romans.

Michael Fishbane: I essentially agree with Robert Wilken. The main evidence for interconnection between the communities, in many cases, must be reconstructed from exegetical features found in the Talmud, Midrash, and Patristic literature. In many intriguing cases, formulations appear to be responses to a theological position taken by Jews or Christians. A case in point is the commentary on the Song of Songs in *Songs Rabba* and in the writings of Origen. Various scholars have noting several intriguing points where it would appear that the Jews have responded to a Christian claim or vice versa. Caesaria of the early third century would have been a hospitable occasion for such contacts.

Evidence for contact may also be found in the preservation of lost Jewish exegeses in early and later Patristic literature. Louis Ginzberg amply demonstrated that much of value was preserved in this way. And not just in an anonymous or hidden way. Jerome, for example, often begins his citations of Jewish comments with the words, "as the Hebrews say," and we also know that he was tutored by a Jewish scholar. It would not be wise to exaggerate such contacts in antiquity; nor would it be wise to ignore them.

Audience member: Is there a parallel in Christian thought to living in the Land being a mitzvah?

Robert Wilken: Well, there are some parallels, but I do not think they should be pushed. Certainly it would not be some kind of obligation or law, nothing of that sort. The most impressive case is a passage that comes from the life of one of these Palestinian monks. The biographer says that he had come from Cappadocia, in Asia Minor. He had come to live in the land of Israel near Jerusalem as a fufillment of biblical prophecy in Isaiah. And he was the first Christian to use the term "Holy Land" for the region around Jerusalem. Now he does not say which passage from Isaiah he has in mind. I think probably what he has in mind are passages that speak of the desert becoming a blooming city, and there are several possibilities that could be used there. So that would be a case where there is a clear sense that living in the land is a fulfillment of prophecy. But that is somewhat rare.

The other instances, as I said before, are monks who have come to the Holy Land because of Jerusalem and the holy places. One of the characteristics in Palestinian monasticism, in contrast to, say, Egyptian or Syrian monasticism, is that they are mostly people who have come from elsewhere to live in the land because they feel that living there puts them into immediate contact with the holy places.

And then they use the verse from Genesis 12, "Go up to the land that I will show you." So there is that kind of understanding. Later, as Christians become the defenders of the land and bury their dead there, they identify with the land as part of their own historical memory. Then you get biblical texts about, for example, Job being buried with his fathers, and so the same language is used about others. It is very interesting about the Crusades, a much-maligned period in Christian history, because of such a prejudice that has developed over it. Last June I was in Jerusalem for a conference on Jerusalem, and a scholar from Hebrew University named Amnon Linder read a paper on the religious and spiritual roots of the Crusades. He actually had found Christian liturgical texts, and they expressed a form of Christian Zionism. It was the same logic, the same texts, the same understanding as that of the Jews—Christians now wanting to regain what was once theirs, which is the logic of Zionism. It was an extraordinary paper. I am not myself a scholar of that period, but I knew such texts had to be there. It turned up in Latin manuscripts in places that that no one had ever noticed before. So the parallels can be developed.

Audience member: Judaism has a passion for the physical city of Jerusalem. How central is that for the Jewish state?

Michael Fishbane: Judaism is not one thing, and Jews do not believe one thing. There is an enormous range of attitudes. One of the issues that I tried to emphasize was that Jerusalem becomes a spiritual symbol for the attachment to the land, and a longing for the restoration of Zion and the Temple. I also stressed that spiritual images developed in Judaism alongside more concrete ones, and that the symbolic features never displaced the reality or importance of the earthly Jerusalem. Thus, however much certain medieval philosophers or mystics emphasized the spiritual and symbolic aspects of Jerusalem, the concreteness of the city was always a feature of halakhic discourse, and messianic yearnings always included the physical aspect of the event as an essential component.

Audience member: Jerusalem is a city holy not just to two traditions but to a third tradition as well, namely, Islam. How did we get to the situation today where Jerusalem is a virtual tinderbox?

Michael Fishbane: As I indicated in my remarks, we face a new challenge. The challenge is to try to overcome certain forms of exclusivity that it is only one or the other. The ecumenical spirit tries to transcend the exclusive domination or claim, which may have substance in terms of medieval discussions in which the issue of absolute truth that would exclude other groups may have been part of the climate. The challenge in modern theory is to rise above that kind of rhetoric and to find the religious language that honors the intense spiritual commitment of these three faiths to Jerusalem and tries to find a way in which there will be space for the spiritual and physical presence of all who want to dwell there. This is not easy, because of historical situations and historical conditions and memories and concerns. But the issue is to try to be focused on the moral recentering which would begin that process, rather than on the claims of exclusive legitimacy.

Robert Wilken: One of the things that we as Westerners and Americans forget is that Arab does not mean Muslim. There is an Arabic-speaking Christian tradition which is the indigenous Christian tradition in Israel, in Palestine and the West Bank and in Syria and the region. In thinking about political, social, and religious questions, it is important to make the distinction and to realize that there are Christian Arabs, and to realize they are caught in a situation in which it is difficult for them to be understood on either side. The Western Christians who go there do not realize that there is such a thing as a Christian Arab. The Muslim Arabs have difficulty, as the Arab countries become more nationalistic, to see the Christians as part of the Arab community. So they find themselves beleaguered from both sides, and the Western Christians turn out in many cases not to be their friends in terms of their relationship to the governments in the Middle East. It is a significant problem because of their own self-understanding and their long attachment to places, the cities, towns.

One of the stories I tell in my book is about a little village near Bethlehem now being surrounded by new settlements. It would be close to Gilo in new Jerusalem. In the Middle Ages a French pilgrim came through the region, and he wanted to buy wine to take with him to go down to Mount Sinai. He said he could not find wine among the Saracens, as he put it, that is, among the Muslims. But he discovered that there was a Christian village, Beit Jala, and they produced wine, and he said that it was very good wine. Well, to this day it is still a Christian village, and it is still producing wine. So the self-understanding of these Christian people is going to be quite different from that of the Jew who comes from elsewhere or the Israeli or the Arab Muslim in terms of their relationship to the place.

Audience member: Since the Christians were lamenting the destruction of Jerusalem by the Persians in the year 614, where were the Christian lamentations for the destruction of the Second Temple in the year 70 of the first century?

Robert Wilken: I think that is the point, isn't it? I think there are two ways to answer the question. One is to say that there was a different relation to the city at that time than there was at a later point, and that insofar as they lamented, Christians lamented as Jews, and that those texts would be among what we now call the Jewish apocryphal writings. But the other side of it, I think, is simply to recognize that we have no texts that come from the early Jewish–Christian communities. The only texts that we have come from that part of the early Christian community that had gone in a different direction from that of the Jewish Christians.

In other words, that we do not have texts could be partly an explanation. The reason there are Christian lamentations over Jerusalem is because the Christian affection that developed, drawing of course on Jewish sources, was a result of Christians actually living in the city.

Abraham Joshua Heschel: Prophet of Social Activism

November 10, 1997

John Healey: Fordham University is privileged to be able to join with the Jewish community tonight in honoring the memory of Rabbi Abraham Joshua Heschel. Rabbi Heschel is justly regarded as one of the great modern spokespersons for the Jewish religious tradition. His study of the prophets, his writings on prayer and Sabbath obvservance and on "God's search for man" have, however, been received also as somehow "ours" in the Christian community. Indeed, he is cited over and over in Christian writings on spirituality as a truly "rabbinic" authority.

Tonight it is not just the spirituality of Rabbi Heschel we wish to honor but also his own living out of the prophet's vocation. At a time of political and social turmoil in our country, Rabbi Heschel spoke out courageously when such speech was as risky— and as challenged—as it was in the days of Amos and Isaiah. Just as courageously, he reached out to Christian friends, worked with them, and invited them to the intimacy of his Sabbath dinner at a time when Jews and Christians were still learning to speak with each other.

We have come a long way from those early days of dialogue, and these annual *Nostra Aetate* sessions are evidence of just how far we have come. But if Christians and Jews are able now to speak honestly to each other in a spirit of growing friendship, it is because of those who reached out to each other in a shared commitment to justice when that took a prophet's courage. Of those forerunners, none stands higher than Rabbi Abraham Joshua Heschel.

Eugene B. Borowitz: Abraham Heschel's significant role in the protest movements against our sinful racial laws and practices, and against the evil of our waging war in Vietnam, are well enough known that twenty-five years after his death we gather in these numbers to remember and celebrate his life. Not as widely known but still unforgotten is his role in helping awaken the American Jewish community to the spiritual genocide practiced against the Jews of the Soviet Union. If, today, Abraham Heschel is one of American Jewry's mythic heroes, it is because of what he stood for and what he then did about it in the troubled social circumstances of his maturity. I only add to this record that he was my teacher at the Hebrew Union College in Cincinnati during the second half of his near six years there. Though we had only sporadic contact after that, we maintained a warm relationship that allowed us to resume communication instantly whenever our paths later crossed.

I am grateful to Fordham University for its kind invitation to participate in this fifth annual dialogue carrying forward the message of *Nostra Aetate* and to do so by sharing a platform with Fr. Dan Berrigan, himself a mythic figure of imposing stature, though one happily still with us. Fr. Berrigan has had his own strong influence upon me as upon so many others, even though we have never met before this evening. But no one alive to the ethical issues of securing and maintaining a moral world in our time could fail to be challenged by the prophetic initiatives which he and his brother and their courageous colleagues have undertaken over the years. In his presence, as in hearing about him over the years, I am again made anxious about how well I have lived up to what I have taught and why I have often acted with timidity when moral boldness probably was required. Thus by his life he too has been my teacher and that of many others, a goodness that I am happy to have the privilege of acknowledging to him before this community.

Thinking about these two great figures suggested to me, perhaps because of the mood of self-examination they evoked in me, that I might best contribute to our discussion by ruminating on two concurrent themes. Mostly I should like to speculate on what, for all their comradely ethical passion, made Abraham Heschel take a somewhat different approach from that of Fr. Berrigan to acting on the imperatives of the prophets. Doing this will also allow me to make some generalizations about the path of Jewish ethics as a whole.

My principal theme came to me when, as I thought back over those now rapidly receding exciting times, I could not recall an occasion when Dr. Heschel went to jail for one of the great causes to which he dedicated himself. When I checked that impression with his biographer, Samuel Dresner, I was told that my memory had not failed me in this matter. Sam also reminded me that shortly before he died, Dr. Heschel had been among those who waited outside the Danbury federal prison to greet Fr. Philip Berrigan on his release from his most recent sentence. I am ill-equipped to analyze why most members of his order and of his church, indeed most Christian ethicists generally, did not emulate Fr. Berrigan's interpretation of Christian duty in those years. However, I can say something about how my teacher's theology and the thrust of Jewish ethics generally led him to his more law-abiding approach.

What is at stake in this divided sense of duty is our response to the example and teaching of the prophets, those extraordinary teachers, on our obligations to other people as a critical aspect of our responsibility to God. In the preferred interpretation of Jewish and Christian thinkers, it is the prophets who most clearly enunciate the ethical thrust of biblical faith, particularly as it relates to our societies. Their standards are so exalted and compelling that living up to them has long been a major trial for believers; thus, the devastating critique they directed to their own generation has turned out to be a timeless rebuke and inspiration to those who attend to God speaking through their words. Difficult enough as these prophetic messages are for us, we are far more perplexed by the example they set of how to overcome the stubborn resistance of their community. Many of them were moral provocateurs, conscious violators of community convention, wild-men unable to stop acting out their impulse to proclaim God's truth and get people to live by it. A false prophet like Zedekiah goes around with iron horns on his head (1Kings 22:11); a relative insider like Isaiah summons Judah's leaders to hear that he is calling his newly born son *Maher-Shalal-Hash-Baz*, which is more a political statement than a name (Isaiah 8:1–3); Jeremiah variously does symbolic acts with loin cloths (ch. 13), potter's ware (ch. 19), a real estate purchase (ch. 32),and the wearing of a yoke around his neck (ch. 27); Hosea marries a whore

(Hosea 1:2–3); and Ezekiel, who may be the consummate virtuoso of bizarre symbolism, not only lies down for over a year to
simulate the coming siege of Jerusalem but manages to get God
to agree that during that demonstration he should not have to
cook his bread over dry human feces but can do so with cow
dung (Ezekiel 4:1–15). If God's command fills one's soul today in
some way as it did the prophets and if the sins of one's society are
as egregious as those of ancient Israel, should we too not be
moved to strong action? Moreover, since we can do so much
more damage to one another than they could, and since we, unlike them, have grown up with the Bible and communal traditions of living its precepts, should we not know better than they
did what constitutes sin? And should we too not then be moved
to do acts of prophetic outrageousness so that God's demands will
no longer be ignored? Something like that, I surmise, moved Fr.
Berrigan and his colleagues to their acts of defiant but non-violent
moral witness.

If I recall correctly, though a number of Jews joined the cam-
paigns involving acts of civil disobedience, some going to jail for
it, Jews were not attracted in notable numbers to religiously motivated acts of high ethical symbolism. In part that is because the
Jerry Rubins and Abbie Hoffmans of that time were essentially
secular in their orientation, believing that, at best, activist ethics
was all that remained lasting in Jewish teaching. But Abraham
Heschel identified just that modernist confidence in the self, its
secure reliance on its own reason and conscience, as the root idol-
atry of our time. His works brim with his imaginative, learned,
insightful efforts to make God the central reality of our lives. And
his oft-commented upon inimitable literary style, one so uniquely
inspiring that it still speaks evocatively to fresh readers today, is
exquisitely suited to his goal of raising us out of our dogmatic
secularity and opening us up to the reality of God and God's
revelation.

Why, then, was so God-centered a teacher as Abraham Heschel
not moved to perform acts of prophetic provocation? I think the
answer we may presume to give to that question must grow from
his unique understanding of the prophets and that, in turn, must
be set within the greater context of traditional Judaism's attitude
toward civic responsibility.

If Dr. Heschel's primary concern was to restore consciousness of the independent reality of God to modern Judaism, its immediate corollary was the restoration of the reality of revelation. In all the theories of modern Judaism that preceded Dr. Heschel's, human initiative had been substituted for God's action. Thus Hermann Cohen, Leo Baeck, and Mordecai Kaplan, in their various fashions, substituted human discovery for God's input to humans. They stretched human reason as far as to suggest that some people are genuinely inspired, a humanistic notion that only substitutes surprise at the exceptional for the more mundane notions of human growth or evolution. Even Martin Buber, and similarly Franz Rosenzweig, who spoke of relationship with a real God— one not ourselves, though allowing for independent Divine input—made human beings so important a factor in the process that, from Dr. Heschel's point of view, both God's stature and the authority of what had been communicated were compromised. Already in his doctoral dissertation at the University of Berlin, later reworked as the 1936 book *Die Prophetie*, he had striven to explain the reality of prophecy in Western intellectual terms. Specifically, he utilized phenomenological categories to indicate the believability, perhaps even the truth, of the prophetic insistence that they spoke God's words for God and not out of their own genius. God had, in fact, revealed the Divine will to human kind. Revelation was as real as it had all along claimed to be and Dr. Heschel was the champion of its credibility.

Contrast this Heschelian neo-traditionalism with what prior modern Jewish theologians had made of revelation. For them, following the leadership of Hermann Cohen, the prophets were the heroes of eternal Judaism because they had the first clear insight into the mandatory nature of ethics and its universal reach. As Leo Baeck put it, the essence of Judaism is its universal ethics, one any rational human being might come to know but which was first given lasting historic power and social sweep by the Jewish people and its devotion to this humanizing idea. Prophetic Judaism, as many ideologues began to term it, was the Judaism of ethical dedication. From this notion stemmed the unparalleled participation of modern Jews in every movement for human betterment in which they were permitted to take a role. Even as they secularized, Jews disproportionately retained this commitment to ethics.

For modernized Jews, then, the prophets were still of interest as superb teachers of ethics, mostly because they went beyond face-to-face righteousness and spoke of what would constitute a society acceptable to God. In a day when democracy had made social policy a matter of every citizen's concern and when the vagaries of history kept raising new challenges and opportunities for humanizing our collective existence, prophetic Judaism was a vision of telling relevance. Of course, it could easily degenerate into mere exhortations to civility or an acceptable means for furthering the self-interest of Jews in securing their status by hiding behind a concern with all minority rights. Nonetheless, no matter how great the evasions or mix of motives, ethics became the passion of the modernized Jewish community in a manner that still manifests itself today.

For Dr. Heschel that limited reading of the prophets reinforced the sin of modernity in replacing God with human reason and reducing the full scope of the Torah's commandments to doing good to one another. His two great systematic statements of the 1950s, Man is Not Alone and God in Search of Man, have almost no extended discussion of ethics—an unheard of reading of Jewish duty in those days. I said "almost" because there is a passage in Man is Not Alone which deals with the topic and it is entitled "The Inadequacy of Ethics." There Dr. Heschel inveighs against the inadequacy of the reigning Jewish understanding of ethical responsibility which spoke of it in the rationalistic neo-Kantian terms of Hermann Cohen. He finds this philosophic construal of ethics false to the realities of human existence and oblivious to the human proclivity to sin. I do not think that his reticence at discussing Jewish ethics in these works should be seen as anything more than his polemic against what he considers the current minimalization of what God requires of us. And it is to that broader vision of Jewish duty that he devotes himself and his message. Within it, he has no hesitation in speaking positively of the need to do what is ethical, even if all his mentions of it are tangential to his larger purpose.

It is only in his 1962 volume, The Prophets, that he allows himself a full-scale statement of God's requirement of us to do good to others. It does not come in his treatment of the seven individual prophets he first devotes himself to. Only after establishing his understanding of the broad reach of their message, and particularly of the validity of their claims that this is, in fact, God's message, does he move on to present a substantial thematic discussion of justice—both the justice of God and its implications for human action. Here, finally, does the full Heschelian devotion to what others call ethics manifest itself. Amos and the prophets who followed him not only stressed the primacy of morality over sacrifice, but even proclaimed that "the worth of worship, far from being absolute, is contingent upon moral living, and that when immorality prevails, worship is detestable" (p. 195). "The greater masterpiece still undone, still in the process of being created, is history. For accomplishing His grand design, God needs the help of man. Man is and has the instrument of God, which he may or may not use in consonance with the grand design. Life is clay, and righteousness the mold in which God wants history to be shaped. . . . God needs mercy, righteousness; His needs cannot be satisfied in the temples, in space, but only in history, in time. . . . Justice is not an ancient custom, a human convention, a value, but a transcendent demand, freighted with divine concern. It is not only a relationship between man and man, it is an *act* involving God, a divine need. . . . It is not one of His ways, but in all His ways" (p. 198). The temptation to go on citing him is great indeed and, summoning more strength than I can often muster, I resist it.

Of course Dr. Heschel was deeply, passionately devoted to what most other Jews, less theistically oriented and with much narrower horizons of Jewish duty, called "ethics." For both of them that involved feeling as much as it did mind, the mercy and compassion which the rabbis taught were primary characteristics of the Jew. And it involved a sense of commandment—in the Kantian language, a categorical imperative, though Dr. Heschel insisted on acknowledging its transcendent source to be the word and will of God. Where they differed, and it was no small matter, was the issue of context. His predecessor modern thinkers believed that the ethical impulse set the bounds within which all Jewish duty was to be evaluated and in which our understanding of God was to be shaped. Dr. Heschel insisted that God's revelation to the prophets alone should determine what constitutes Jewish duty.

But now, having taken you this winding intellectual way, I can, I believe, state my explanation of his civilly obedient dedication to acts of righteousness. The biblical prophets did their acts of spiritual provocation because God had told them to do so; they often complied reluctantly and grudgingly, doing what they sometimes considered thankless, impractical, and even personally repulsive acts, because they knew that was what God wanted them to do. Dr. Heschel believed that people in our time, Jew or non-Jew, might equally have so intense a relationship with God that they could hear the Divine behest to do something similar today. But because it did not happen to him, because God never called him to be a prophet, only *nebbich,* a Jewish teacher, he did not do such acts himself.

And in that understanding, let me now much more briefly add, he was reflecting the vast bulk of Jewish teaching and experience in this area. Recall, please, that after the first century C.E., Jews increasingly lived as minorities in Diaspora communities. Though not always persecuted there, they were a people apart, social inferiors, and thus, often, severely discriminated against. (The record is much darker in many places as the centuries became millennia.) Jewish law had to take this new embattled social posture into consideration and in early Talmudic times it did so through its doctrine of *dina demalkhuta dina,* the rule that, for Jews, the civil law of the state carries the authority of Torah law. One major qualification of this rule is relevant here: that it must be a just state, and the criterion for this is whether in legal matters it treats Jews as it does all other citizens. Naturally, over the centuries and the diverse polities and economic orders in which Jews found themselves living, there were special interpretations of this principle. But it has remained relatively stable down to the present day. Jewish law demands respect for a reasonably just society and Jewish prudence, reinforced by a long history of exclusion and discrimination, powerfully reinforces that attitude. As a result, over the fifteen hundred or so years that Jews have lived by *dina demalkhuta dina* we have only the rarest evidence that they have thought God commanded them to confront their governments and by their unconventional acts to pass judgment upon them.

Only in the last two centuries has the spread of democracy given the broad mass of people a say in who rules them and how they are to do so. It thus authorized, even encouraged, new forms of critique and action. As societies grudgingly opened themselves up to Jews and other outsiders, the possibility of Jewish action against the government became a significant reality. Characteristically, Jews in free societies have largely supported the political forces seeking to secure everyone's rights and to expand their effective freedom, but most Jews have shied away from the radical groups who sought to do this by revolution. In the minority that leaned strongly to the left there were far more Jewish socialists than communists, though the latter certainly got more public attention. The American labor movement, in contrast to its European forebears, rejected becoming a political party and concentrated instead on working for the improvement of wages and working conditions, an ethos for which authorities deem its leader, Samuel Gompers, largely responsible and who, others have suggested, had deep roots in the tradition of Jewish social prudence.

I am suggesting that Abraham Heschel's passionate ethical activism grew out of the twin strands of the revealed law reinforced by the lingering pains of Jewish experience. For Dr. Heschel, Moses is, as the Torah says, the greatest of the Jewish prophets and Jewish law is the heart of God's revelation. The *halakhah* commands with God's authority behind it even though its dialectical development is carried out through human initiative. When one reads his rhapsodic treatment of the holy deed as the place where God and humans meet, one needs to include *dina demalkhuta dina*. Surely that principle has special force for American Jews who live in a Diaspora equality unique in Jewish history and unparalleled anywhere in the world today. And, if I may now express my own sentiments, when one has seen German democracy authorize the murder of most of one's family and countless others, it is blasphemous to suggest that, as was suggested in those days, that this country should now be called *Amerika,* and not honored as the one nation courageous enough to keep expanding its freedom to one pariah group after another. Dr. Heschel found ways to respond to what he knew was God's unceasing imperative to do something about injustice and he had a powerful effect then and now on American Jews as well as on many other citizens, believers and unbelievers alike. He was not called to be a prophet, but few in our time have set a better example of what it means to be a caring Jew and a spiritual heir of the prophets.

Daniel Berrigan: Great memories and ironies swirl about me. I came on the following from Rabbi Heschel very early on; he spoke the words shortly before the Second World War. In February 1938, Heschel was called upon to expound his understanding of the impending war. Martin Buber had been invited to address a group of Quaker leaders by his friend, Rudolph Schlosser, a German Quaker and pacifist. But that evening, Buber was overcome by influenza and designated Heschel to speak in his place. "Buber's assistant," as Heschel was known, interpreted the historical moment in theological terms. Entitled *Seeking a Meaning*, his speech opened dramatically with a symbolic scene: "Carried over the gates of the world in which we live are the weapons of the demons. It is happening in our time that the peoples are forging their sickles into swords and their scythes into spears. And by inverting the prophetic words entirely, the people turn away from the words that come from Zion."[1]

This remains a striking image in light of the current prison status of my Jesuit colleague, Stephen Kelly, and of my brother Philip, in enacting that command from Isaiah: "Beat your swords into plowshares." I was delighted to learn that that image was so much a part of the early intellectual and spiritual equipment of Heschel.

Friendship says everything with regard to Heschel and myself. I began to seek enlightenment upon the history of friendship, and came upon a rather illuminating, very old quote from Aristotle: "Friendships are possible only to those of virtue. Capacity for friendship is indeed the most accurate measure of virtue. It is also the foundation of a state. For great legislators are more for friendship than for justice" (*Nicomachean Ethics*, Book VIII).

I think a connection is drawn here, and tightened. And I question: Is friendship the foundation of the state? We have precious

---

[1] Cited in Edward K. Kaplan, *Holiness in Words: Abraham Joshua Heschel's Poetics of Piety* (Albany: State University of New York Press, 1996), Appendix B.

few examples today of such a view. We have rather an opposite principle virulently active: Betrayal is the foundation of the state. Betrayal of the truth, betrayal of one another, betrayal of outsiders and minorities, of expendable people, as in the instances of Nicaragua, Salvador, Guatemala, Vietnam, Iraq, and Cuba. Many perish, according to this dictum. A kind of suave ruthlessness, an icy incapacity of heart marks American authority in the world, at large and at home.

I note at work yet another gloss on the principle of Aristotle, not altogether an improvement. He declared, "Great legislators care more for friendship than for justice." The current principle, I think, is grossly Machiavellian. It goes something like this: Wicked legislators care more for betrayal than they do for justice. Is there in anyone's immediate memory an example of a person of authority in our country sacrificing great power for the sake of friendship? I must confess I know of nonesuch.

I have other far different examples at hand, and with great pain report them. The road to political victory today is paved with corpses and victims. Its stages are marked by friendships given over and wasted. Trust is betrayed, bargains are struck, ideals are lost on the wind. And those who gather after the moral massacre and stand rejoicing with the delinquent winner voice no objection to such conduct. How could they? They have everything to gain by it. What these victors of our days substitute for the friends they gave over is something other: cronyism, nepotism, back room deals, huge sacks of loot, and eventually and inevitably, betrayal on a much larger scale—socialized betrayal declaring entire peoples expendable.

Aristotle, though, came on a stunning truth, as I would understand it. Personal affections are bound up with a commonweal, or a common woe. This is a high leap of moral imagination—one worthy of respect perhaps all the more so because it is so seldom honored in behavior. The neglect and contempt and outright denial offered his principle are a measure of the distance we have traveled in reverse gear, far from a vision of humanity anciently celebrated.

I have an objection to register about Aristotle's comment. For him, great legislators care more for friendships than for justice. I cannot for the life of me, and in the light of Heschel, see that friendship can correctly be set over against justice, as though honoring the one would imply, even in extreme circumstances, dishonoring the other. As far as I can understand, the honoring of friendship is a high, perhaps the highest, form of justice. And further, if the two are even hypothetically put at odds, each is put at risk.

The theme of friendship has faded, as many have noted, in the literature of our era. It cannot hold a candle to the consistent flurry over all sorts of other engrossing—I would venture to say, distracting—subjects. We have lost a great deal in our frenzy after technique, even the technique of sexuality. Perhaps sorriest of all, we have risked losing one another.

On the American scene, one of the last essayists who treated friendship is Emerson ("Friendship," *Essays*: First Series). He sees fragility and lack of endurance in any friendship that does not include "some greater universal fraternity"—again, Heschel comes to mind. But the fraternity named America is in danger of dissolution, and there is left to us a world of furiously competing hostilities gathered behind a palisade spiked with nuclear tipped weapons, a world that has become a kind of universal suicide club.

There is another loss up close adduced by our seer Emerson. That loss of "one another" is not solely the loss implied in savage wars abroad. It is the domestic loss of American by American, of light skin and dark, sex and its opposite or its like, and so on. I mean to include every variation and celebration and harmony and dissonance of the human, loss of what Hopkins celebrated, "the roll, the rise, the carol, the creation."

Isaiah, that favorite of Heschel, spoke of the God who ironically knows something about our politics and their consequence, something of which, generation after generation, we remain so ignorant. This: God, as he implied, had only to leave imperialists to their own devices. Give us time. Give us one war too many. Give us ever more piratical economics. We will bring ourselves down. In the meantime, as Isaiah says bluntly, the domestic scene will be a horror, marked by conflict within the soul and the body politic: "I will rouse Egypt against Egypt, brother against brother, neighbor against neighbor, city against city, realm against realm" (Isaiah 19:2ff.).

Emerson, for his part, insists on certain crucial connections. He sees them as primordial, forged in the very emergence of the human—the personal joined with the social, the mystical with the political, the friend at distance, the friend up close. The tragedy, as he implied, is the severing of these one from another, and the consequent alienation and enmity within and without. I do not call this Emersonian sense of connection merely pragmatic. It appears to me as a simple matter of biology, the capacity of spirit to develop its own entropy; which is to say that personal friendship is a call to friendship with all. I need not add that Martin Luther King has expressed it well; the call in our generation is no longer a matter of levity or romanticism, or even a choice among choices. It is a strict mandate of survival. We shall love one another or die, as Auden writes.

Emerson, I submit, was right. The measure of our humanity is the fostering of friendship, a phrase rightly implying a laborious task, both of building community and resisting socialized death. To make friends with all the living, to make friends with enemies and the stranger at the gate, the "undocumented," the "illegal," with street people, mental patients, those at the bottom of the imperial pyramid, the despised and feared and forgotten; friendship with criminals and yuppies and tyrants and victims: this is the task. A. J. Muste, a peacemaker of the stature of Heschel, scandalized the peace movement of the Second World War by declaring, "If I cannot love Hitler, I cannot love anyone."

By making friends, I submit, we banish former labels and stigmas, and we confer on ourselves and other unlikely specimens a new and noble name. Friend—a word variously forbidden, stigmatized, denounced, and prosecuted. In the Prophets, in the New Testament, a word still awaiting embodiment. A word meantime to be created in bunkers and bases, in places given over to enmity, namelessness, irresponsibility, and death. A name to be created also in jails and courts and death rows, and among the aged and ill, endangered by medicals gone mad, in abortion clinics and inhuman warehouses. We shall undertake this work as Heschel invited, or we shall all likewise perish.

I remember Abraham, a man of prayer, and a man on the line; this, simply put, was my friend. Across vectors of insight and moral effort, he walked gracefully and at cost. I passed, and we met; for me, it was providential. Our first meeting included a Protestant minister. The time was 1965, the occasion a press conference to express the revulsion of at least a minority in the religious community in the face of Johnson's war in Vietnam. The press arrived and we delivered our words. Then, the task of the moment done with, two of us prepared to depart, knowing as we did that we had done what we could, knowing as well that by no means available to any of us could we end the war.

The minister and I rose in our places, a hand was laid firmly on our arms, and the voice of Heschel was in our ears. A word uttered with great urgency: "Are we then finished? We depart content, while the war goes on?" We should have known the question was quintessential Heschel, which is to say it contained its own answer. And it awaited ours. We did not go home. We sat again, we three, and of that gesture of the rabbi, both simple and crucial, a community was born. It came to be known as "Clergy Concerned about the War." It perhaps goes without saying that in the beginning we were hardly inundated with proffers or contributions or new members. As Abraham would say ruefully, "We should have called ourselves 'Clergy Unconcerned.' Then you would see them flock to us."

My own fortunes worsened. Under mysterious ecclesiastical marching orders, I was ordered out of the country in the fall of 1965, bound for Latin America, a one-way airline ticket in hand. Meantime, "Clergy Concerned" mounted a New York meeting against the war. I was told later that in a liturgical gesture initiated by Heschel, an empty chair was set on stage, signifying my enforced absence. When a dignitary attempted to occupy it, Heschel gravely gestured him elsewhere. The war worsened, as wars do. By now it bore its own momentum, rolling relentlessly onward. Meantime, what lives and fortunes were not being borne under!

Another era, another story. For a time during the Israeli–Egyptian conflict of 1967 it was as though a shadow fell across our friendship. I asked myself, would Heschel object to this war as he had objected to Vietnam? Away from New York that summer and heartsick with thought of my friend, I wrote him a questioning letter. Then second thoughts intruded. His health had declined drastically, and I had no heart to raise an issue bound to be painful. I tore up the letter.

In the spring of 1968 I voyaged to Hanoi to recover American prisoners of war. There, like any Vietnamese peasant, I cowered under the bombardment of, so to speak, my own airforce. It was a momentous education, and I learned a lesson. After returning within a few months, I joined seven other unvanquished spirits in the burning of draft files in Catonsville, Maryland. During those terrible years, Heschel, too, was learning, and quickly. He moved from civil rights to anti-war work. More and more was demanded of his time and his emotional reserves. He aged visibly. By 1972, when I returned to New York after a stint in prison, it was dolorously clear to friends and family that he was ill indeed.

I referred to Abraham earlier as a man of prayer. Is the insistence, I ask myself, redundant, discipline being one with religious faith in any tradition? Perhaps not. In those days of fervent war and perfervid anti-war, public acknowledgment of one's faith, even among friends, was by no means usual. One's politics were public property, sometimes in a crass sense. One's faith was another matter, almost a matter of embarrassment. One marched in the light, but one believed in a corner. The dichotomy was for the most part distressingly adolescent.

In this matter of unashamed faith, publicly acknowledged, Heschel was at odds as usual. With him, tradition stood against fashion. One knew where he stood, as for example, one knew where Martin Luther King stood. Their faith was consistent, lucid, intense, and political. They and their like announced God in God's world, God suffering and rejoicing amid people, the people acknowledging God's sovereignty in passionate quest for justice and peace, in prayer and in worship. Faith and life in the world—it was all one, a hyphenated reality. It was to be proclaimed in the image of the prophets, "from the housetops."

Was the world attending, meantime, to Heschel, and mending its ways? Or was the world rushing ignorantly in its course, paying no heed, condemning the prophetic word? To Heschel, no matter the outcome, one simply went on. Faith was its own credential. Faith stood there, spoke up, and paid up. This was the faith of Heschel as I understood it, and I dare say of the community that gathered round him to pray and make peace in a bad time. The winds of misfortune that scattered so many and destroyed so many, those same winds also brought unlikely people to one another's side, standing and walking together. This was our great good fortune, amid much tragedy. We discovered one another and so "doubled the heart's might"

During that time, I was given a great privilege, which the Heschel family will perhaps recall, to assist at seder in the Heschel apartment. I was warmly received. The food was excellent, prayers of intercession were uttered: for an end of war, for the peace that passes understanding, for the victims of war (the American dead being our chief import in those horrid days). And who could calculate the numbers of Vietnamese, Cambodian, and Laotian dead? We prayed for the victims everywhere; these were Heschel's fervent prayers, and mine also. This, I thought exultantly on the way home later that evening, this was an ecumenism I could take seriously.

I see him at table vividly, his bearded head bowing and rising in prayer. It was as though he was wrapped into the *shekinah*, the *mysterium tremendum*. I know no better way of putting it: he knew how to pray. In a gathering of family and friends, or in attendance at the majestic Second Vatican Council, it made little difference. He lived before God.

Great suffering attended his last days. And for better or worse I was there. Indeed, it might be adduced, and was at the time, that I became an element of his suffering. The war, the war; it bled our youth, our innocence, our religion, our freedom. The war was an albatross which Kennedy bore until it bore him under. Then a weight beyond bearing, the war was lowered like a horrid dalmatic of office onto the shoulders of Johnson. The war became both an emblem and a legacy. No president could die intestate; each must inherit.

The war rotted and clung and festered and stank to high heaven. It became Nixon's war. But all this was in the future. There was an election at stake; Nixon narrowed his vision like a gimlet, to win, as they say, by hook or by crook. His genius was, above all, opportunistic. He concocted, for example, a specious devotion to the prospering of Israel. In private, as the famous tapes bear witness to his degraded mind, the character of his "devotion" is quite clear. Devotion? A matter of principle? It is inordinately difficult to attach such words implying moral alertness and compassion to such a phenomenon. In any case, Nixon won the prize upon which he had staked everything. And what could the future hold for those who saw in the political landscape only disaster and humiliation?

I sought out my friend more frequently in his closet of an office, cluttered with tomes, at the Jewish Theological Seminary. I was an ex-prisoner, an ex-prisoner of war, so to speak. I was also, as was my friend Abraham, more and more isolated in America. It could not be denied that Nixon was a genius of sorts, master of the bloody tradeoff, contriving to amity with people of common cause, and so in effect winning them to his side. Israel or Vietnam? The question cut across boundaries and religious traditions. It cut to the bone of our community, what remained of it. Continued support of Israel, continued assault on Vietnam? Could we choose one at the price of the other? What were my friend and I to do?

I proposed a newspaper advertisement stating a united religious opposition—Jewish and Christian—against Nixon's war. Heschel agreed, and we went about New York seeking financial help from the Jewish community. It perhaps goes without saying, no such help was forthcoming from my community. We came on no help in any case. There would be no advertisement. The Jewish community, among many others, had decided in Nixon's favor. So had the majority of Jewish Theological Seminary faculty and students. And these decisions coincided nicely with the electorate at large—Jews, Catholics, everyone: it was Nixon all the way. Now we, a few Protestants and Catholics and Jews, had become the albatross. But this one could be cast off, and Nixon knew it.

Thus, the last days of Heschel stood solid and tragic and alone, in the prophetic line he had honored. And I reflect ruefully that he resembles us lesser mortals at least in this: Never in his darkest hour did he imagine the tragic days that lay ahead, how literally he, and we, would be required to stand by the hurtful truth of God's word.

There remains a species of cold comfort I have had frequent occasion to reflect on. Abraham Heschel stood in opposition to the crimes of the century, first as the Nazis rampaged through Poland. Then he departed Europe with a hope he had left such crimes behind. Alas, innocence had fled the world. The furies of war flew faster than his passage. It was Mars and no other who stood astride America as the distinguished foreigner landed on our shores.

In his years in America, I would judge, Heschel entered the old age of the patriarch whose name he bore, burden upon burden. There were the civil rights years and the war. And finally, the opposition among his own people. In his last years, immensely revered in every circle except his own, he was denied the dubious honor known among Catholics as premature canonization. Thus, too, he entered the larger human family, an exemplar of our common plight and hope. He was scorned and rejected, even as he was loved beyond measure.

At Christmas 1972, Nixon, we were told, had worked out a deal involving the fate of two notorious prisoners; it was a simple solution innocent of moral content. Both prisoners were to be freed simultaneously, Jimmy Hoffa and my brother Philip. Thus would various constituencies be placated. The news came of Philip's imminent freeing. Abraham approached me. Could he be included in the party that would voyage to Danbury to welcome Philip out of prison? There were complications, he explained. He must perform his devotions en route. Would this be objected to? Far from it, it would be, I averred, our privilege to pray with him. So we set out; he prayed his psalms and we for once were silent and joined his prayer.

Of that memorable day, there remain two photographs in my possession. One was taken in the car en route. The lighting is bright and cold; perhaps the sun was coming up. Heschel sits, his leonine profile grave and recollected, lit with the aura of dawn. Just out of the photograph, his book of devotions lies open. The second photograph was taken that same morning, just after Philip's release. As the crowd pressed around, the two stood face to face, tall man and short. Heschel grasped Philip by the lapels and engaged him fervently, even furiously, eye to eye, head aloft, beard wild in the wind. The figures are frozen in time. One can imagine, if one cannot reconstruct, the passionate welcome and gratitude that welled from Heschel's tongue. All unknowing, and mercifully so, we were nearing the end. That same joyful day on the return to New York we were invited, Philip and myself, to take tea a day or two hence with the Heschel family.

The afternoon arrived. Minutes before we set out across Manhattan, a frantic call reached us. Abraham had been found dead. Would we come quickly? We hurried over. The truth was terrible. Our friend had left this world, having become himself, according to the promise, the father of a multitude, of blessed memory, father and more to me, friend.

I told my soul in gratitude and grief, and still do, how blessed I was that one named Abraham had stood with me for years, in weather fair and foul. And for us foul days far outnumber fair, and a dreadful imbalance in nature and nation might well perdure, or might worsen, or might indeed tip us into chaos. Still, one consolation: One life redeems all. Our world has known another Abraham.

Susannah Heschel: Thank you very much. I am very glad that you have had this program on *Nostra Aetate* at Fordham University for so many years. It is a wonderful program, just as *Nostra Aetate* is a great moment in Western civilization. We should come together and remember it and celebrate it every year. I am very glad that my mother and my husband and I can be with you on this occasion. I have to mention also that my father so much enjoyed lecturing at Catholic universities and seminaries. He used to come home filled with a wonderful sense of joy because he enjoyed the rigor of the intellectual life of the faculty and the students, but he also always had fun at Catholic institutions. The food was delicious and the drink was generous, and he came back in such a happy mood and always enjoyed those invitations.

I have to say how pleased I am to be responding today to Fr. Berrigan and to Rabbi Borowitz. There were two scripture readings in the synagogue on the Sabbath day that my father died. One of them was taken from the Book of First Kings, Chapter 2. King David is on his death bed, and he speaks to Solomon, his son, and tells Solomon to be wary of those who had been David's enemies; but also to take to his heart those who had been his father's friends. And I feel very strongly myself that those who were my father's friends are my friends.

My father devoted many years of his life and energies to the work of the Second Vatican Council and to the statement on Catholic relations with the Jews. He spoke often about the reason why he was involved in this: he did not seek recognition as a Jew, or legitimacy from the church, but he sought rather "the cure from the disease affecting so many minds. That is what we pray for. As a Jew, it is my profound concern that those who worship should be free of contempt for any individual." My father differed in some striking ways from other modern Jewish thinkers who were also very interested in Christianity. You can say that modern Jewish thought is in fact fascinated with Christianity. But in remarkable ways my father is different. For example, he does not discuss Jesus or Paul; he does not write about the New Testament; he does not engage in debates on points of doctrine. He is, rather, interested in helping Catholics be better Catholics. In fact, when he went to see Pope Paul VI, the Pope thanked him for his books for that reason, that they helped young Catholics be better Catholics, and he was so happy that young Catholics were reading my father's books. And that gave my father a great sense of satisfaction. My father asked, what can Jews learn, spiritually, from the great religious traditions of Christianity? That is a question that not enough Jews ask.

I should also mention that my father in those years was not supported by many other Jewish leaders. In fact, there were some who attacked him quite vigorously. I think of Rabbi Norman Lamm and Rabbi Joseph Soloveitchik, and I will just read you one thing that Rabbi Solovechik wrote. He said, "We have no frame of reference for the Christians, not as a culture, and are as far removed from them as we are from Buddhism or any other religion. We cannot communicate with them on the religious level. Our quarrel is with the Jewish people, mainly with many sections of the Reform Rabbis who were ready to betray the Jewish cause for a few Catholic compliments."[2] So I point out to you that although we celebrate my father's work tonight, he often did stand very much alone in his day.

Let me turn first to some of the points that my colleague Professor Borowitz raises. He asks the question why did my father not engage in acts of civil disobedience like Father Berrigan and like the prophets? He answers in a variety of ways. One of the points that I would not completely agree with him about is the question of *dina demalkhuta dina*, "the law of the land is the law,"

---

[2] *The Jewish Horizon*, September–October 1964, p. 4.

namely, that in Rabbinic and post-Rabbinic Judaism, Jews are supposed to be obedient and not violate civil law except in certain circumstances. In fact, there is a second Rabbinic principle, *gezela demalkhuta*, that the kingdom can also commit immoral acts of robbery, and that Jews are enjoined legally, as part of Jewish law, not in any way to participate in the immoral acts of a government, not in any way to benefit from the immoral or illegal acts of a government. So in fact I would say that there is within Rabbinic Judaism itself a mandate upon Jews to commit acts of civil disobedience, disobedience to authority, when their moral conscience commands it.

I remember, from this question of why my father did not commit acts of civil disobedience, what he explained to me in those days. He explained that the question for Fr. Berrigan and for others was, "can I be a free citizen of a country committing atrocities in Vietnam?" The answer was no. My father said that his question for himself was, "How can I use my energies most effectively to bring this war to an end?" He drained his energy going out and speaking and lecturing and participating in demonstrations. And yes, he did follow the example and the teachings of the prophets. They were in fact moral provocateurs, although their provocation was expressed not only through symbolic action but also through their words, through their language. That is a lesson my father followed very carefully. The book that he wrote on the prophets argues that we do not have a dictation theory in Judaism, of God speaking directly to the prophet and the prophet transmitting, unaltered, those words. Rather, there is a prophetic consciousness. There is a religious experience that the prophet has at the moment of revelation; and each prophet has a different experience. It is incumbent upon us also as religious people to develop our inner lives so that when we hear the word of God, we hear it in a way that benefits all people, and we transmit it in a way that benefits the world. It is our consciousness, our inner religious life, that is so important to my father.

He was provocative through words the way Amos was provocative through words and through language. For him language was so central, so important. God created the world through words, and each of our words has the capability of making this a better place or a worse place. For my father what was most important about the prophets was the religious experience they had of outrage. He spoke about the moral passion of the prophets, the sense that the world of injustice was a nightmare for them. He wrote about Vietnam, "it is a burning sin that we remain indifferent." He said that the opposite of good is not evil, the opposite of good is indifference. "What is happening in our own days in America," he wrote, "proves beyond doubt that a strong voice ringing with force and dignity has the power to pierce the iron shield of dormant conscience. What is called for is not a silent sigh, but a voice of moral compassion and indignation, the sublime and inspired screaming of a prophet uttered by a whole community."[3] That was his message and his teaching. Unfortunately, it was not always the whole community that screamed with him.

The other question that Rabbi Borowitz raises, and that I want to simply mention in passing, is the question of why so many young Jews understood their actions in the civil rights movement and opposition to the war in Vietnam in secular terms. I think that was certainly the case for them. For my father that was tragic, and, in fact he blamed Jewish teachers. He wrote when he came back from the march in Selma, Alabama, "I felt again what I had been thinking about for years. The Jewish religious institutions have again missed a great opportunity, namely to interpret a civil rights movement in terms of Judaism. The vast number of Jews participating actively in it are totally unaware of what the movement means in terms of the prophetic tradition."[4] That is what he sought to bring about. He sought to bring to people the religious meaning of social activism, that his political activity could not be divorced from his life of prayer. That is why when he came back from Selma he said, "I felt my legs were praying."[5]

I remember Dan Berrigan very well. He was a good friend of my father's. He often visited us on Shabat and Friday nights, and the delicious food that he remembers from the seder and from Friday night dinners was prepared by my mother, and it was deli-

---

[3] On this subject, Abraham Joshua Heschel, "The Moral Outrage of Vietnam," in Robert McAfee Brown, Heschel, and Michael Novak, *Vietnam: Crisis of Conscience* (New York: Association Press, 1967), pp. 48–61.

[4] Susannah Heschel, ed., *Moral Grandeur and Spiritual Audacity* (New York: Farrar, Straus & Giroux, 1996), Introduction, xxiii–xxiv.

[5] Ibid.

cious always. They were wonderful evenings together at our home. I do not know if he remembers me when I was in high school and junior high, and how I used to debate with him and demand to know why he was—he should forgive me for bringing this up again—why he was so upset about the innocent people in Vietnam who were dying and not about the women who were dying of illegal abortions in this country. I remember arguing with him vociferously about that. My father was kind enough to let me express myself in all of my fourteen-year-old vigor. We felt close to him, very close, so close that in fact I knew he was coming to tea the day my father died, that morning when we woke up, and I called him immediately. That is how close we felt, he was our friend. I remember also that he and my father were planning to write a book or an article in response to Garry Wills's book, *Bare Ruined Choirs* (New York: Dell, 1972). Do you remember that? You never had a chance to do that, in defense of Catholicism.

I agree also that there is far more betrayal in our society than friendship. My father used to say that the reigning commandment is "suspect thy neighbor as thyself." And I suppose here my only disagreement might be over the nature of friendship perhaps, the role of power within friendship, and the notion of loving the enemy in Matthew 5:44. One loves one's enemy, or attempts to do so, but there are still enemies, and Matthew 5 does not take that away, does not say there should not be enemies. You quoted Abraham John Muste, "If I cannot love Hitler I cannot love anyone." It was shocking for me when I first read your essay. I would ask why that is the case, and why it is impossible in fact to discriminate; that in fact I can love and do love many people and I do not love Hitler. I wonder what love means if there exists no hatred, if you simply love everyone. I know that my father did not love Hitler. But I know that he could love very deeply and profoundly. I have to also say that I at the present time am writing about Protestant theologians in Germany who did love Hitler, and whose love for Hitler disgraced Christianity terribly by placing the swastika with the cross on the altar in their churches. My father felt very strongly about friendship that it is reciprocal. He used to tell me a story about a Hasidic Rebbe. Someone came to the Rebbe and said, "Rebbe, I love you so much, I love you so

much." And the Rebbe said, "Tell me, do you know what gives
me pain?" And the man said with eagerness, "Tell me Rebbe, tell
me what gives you pain." And the Rebbe said, "If you don't
know what gives me pain, how can you say that you love me?" I
suppose my father wanted that kind of depth of love in his friendships with people.

If there was one concern, finally, that was absolute to my father,
it was that the Church abandon efforts to convert the Jews. He
called that a spiritual fratricide, an effort to wipe Judaism out of
existence. He said that he would rather go to Auschwitz than give
up his faith. And moreover, he argued forcefully that Christianity
needed Judaism. What meaning does it have for Christians to
speak of the God of Israel if there is no Israel? He emphasized
instead the need for helping one another. So I want to conclude
with his words and his suggestions. He says: "What, then, is the
purpose of interreligious cooperation? It is neither to flatter nor
to refute one another, but to help one another; to share insight
and learning, to cooperate in academic ventures on the highest
scholarly level, and, what is even more important, to search in the
wilderness for wellsprings of devotion, for treasures of stillness, for
the power of love and care for humanity. What is urgently needed
are ways of helping one another in the terrible predicament of
here and now, by the courage to believe that the word of the
Lord endures forever as well as here and now; . . . to cooperate
in trying to bring about a resurrection of sensitivity, a revival of
conscience; to keep alive the divine sparks in our souls; to nurture
openness to the spirit of the Psalms, reverence for the words of
the prophets and faithfulness to the Living God."[6]

Audience member: Professor Heschel, I was very struck in your
introduction to your collection of your father's writings, *Moral
Grandeur and Spiritual Audacity,* with the telegram sent by your
father to President Kennedy in 1963. I would prefer if you told
what that was, but my first question is whether or not you
thought to send that to President Clinton, and what your views
were of the present initiative, once gain, to do something about
race relations in our country.

---

[6] Abraham Joshua Heschel, "No Religion Is an Island" in *Moral Grandeur and
Spiritual Audacity,* pp. 249–50.

Susannah Heschel: Thank you for the question. It is a magnificent telegram that I found among my father's papers and that he sent to President Kennedy, who had invited religious leaders to come to the White House to talk about civil rights. The telegram concludes with a great phrase, which is the title of the book: "The hour calls for moral grandeur and spiritual audacity." I believe that this has been true at many times in our lives since that telegram was sent in 1963, including today. My own personal feeling about the situation today is that I miss what I call the prophetic voices of my father and Martin Luther King, who had visions that they held up to us, that were inspiring and that brought us to tears, because they showed us the possibility of how one can really be a human being, that it is possible to be such a great human being. Nowadays I sometimes hear certain tones of cynicism in people who describe themselves as witnesses, who describe horrors which we need to hear, but I want to hear also some inspiration. I want to be moved also, and stimulated to aspire to something beyond who I am. That would be a reason why that telegram would still be moving today.

Audience member: Today, I think that most people in the Jewish and other religious communities still do not sense the connection between religious meaning and social action, and the imperative to work for social justice, and the notion that we can all be partners with God in the creation of a more just world. Where is the energy—in terms of religious education, interdenominational, ecumenical religious education—where is the impetus, where is it going to come from?

Susannah Heschel: Yes, I believe it is true that my father felt very strongly that what he was doing in his social activism was religious, but it was presented to many people as secular. I think that is beginning to change in part because of a younger generation making it clear what we want. But it is true that many Jewish institutions do not understand, and do still try to keep separate the religious and the secular. It is also true that although there are some theologians who understand, not all of them do. Fr. Berrigan's work and writings and life and activities were not embraced or understood theologically by the Catholic Church, just as my father's were not understood theologically by many Jews. From where does the impetus come? I honestly believe that my father had a tremendous impact on the Jewish community, and I believe very strongly that things are changing in the education the children receive, and in the kinds of rabbis who are in the pulpits today. I do see some change, and it does take a while. But you would not have had, for example, Rabbi Marshall Meyer and his congregation without my father, and that is very important.

Audience member: Professor Heschel, what do you think your father would say about the struggle, at least in the Conservative movement, to bring women and men together not only on the pulpit but also halachically on a more equal ground? I believe this is a moral issue, and have found much resistance to egalitarianism. I do not think your father writes about that, because it was not yet a burning issue in his time.

Susannah Heschel: I am sure Fr. Berrigan remembers that when he visited us at home on Passover at the seder, or on Friday night, my father asked me to lead the prayers, for example, and I had a *Bat Mitzvah* at my request, and an *aliya* for my sixteenth birthday. In our home if we had a *minyan,* women were counted in the *minyan.* My father suggested that I apply to the rabbinical school at the Jewish Theological Seminary, confident that there would be equality very, very soon. So he was in complete agreement with me and with what has become a Jewish feminist movement. I have no concern on that score about where he would stand. Certainly his concern for language, his sensitivity to the words that we use, would have also made him sensitive to the issue of inclusive language.

Audience member: I would like to provide some context for Abraham Heschel's comments about spiritual fratricide, and will end with a question to Professor Heschel. That comment was made during the course of the struggle around *Nostra Aetate,* in which he played a very active role after being brought into that struggle by Rabbi Mark Tanenbaum. He submitted some memoranda to the preparatory commissions of Vatican II, and he was very hopeful. In the penultimate wording of *Nostra Aetate* there was a call for the conversion of the Jews, or something that was interpreted by Jews to be a call for their conversion. Rabbi Heschel became very embittered and angry. When the document was finally adopted, of course, that call for conversion had been changed and a much more open call for all of humanity to find the Lord, to follow the ways of God, was substituted. The document was welcomed by and acceptable to the Jewish community. But I have heard various interpretations of Heschel's response. Was he so embittered by the experience that he was turned off with relations afterward? Or was he mollified by it and was he more positive about it afterward?

Susannah Heschel: I know what you are referring to, and I talk about it briefly in the introduction to the book I edited, *Moral Grandeur.* The very first draft of *Nostra Aetate* was wonderful, and the second one was very disappointing and very upsetting, and my father spoke out forcefully against it and also tried to rally support from other theologians against it. There is a very interesting history to be written here. Eventually there was a compromise, and the hope for the eventual conversion of the Jews was stricken from the final document. My father was very pleased with that. Of course, the final text could have been even stronger, and it would have pleased him much more. But he was never embittered; nor did he ever withdraw from involvement in Jewish–Catholic discussion or from his colleagues at the Vatican. In fact, in 1971, just a year before my father died, he and my mother went to Italy for a lecture tour and he was received by Pope Paul VI. So in fact he was not embittered and he did not withdraw and he continued to maintain good friendships with his Catholic colleagues, as well, of course, with his Protestant colleagues. They were his good friends. I grew up thinking that all Christians were like my parents' friends who came to visit us on Friday night at Sabbath meals. When I got to college I was so surprised to discover that not everyone was like my father's friends.

NOTES ON CONTRIBUTORS

The Rev. Daniel Berrigan, S.J., a well-known social activist, is the author of many books of poetry, essays, and reflections, including *The Trial of the Catonsville Nine* (Boston: Beacon Press, 1970) and, most recently, *And the Risen Bread: Selected Poems, 1957–1997* (New York: Fordham University Press, 1998).

Rabbi Eugene Borowitz is the Sigmund L. Falk Distinguished Professor of Education and Jewish Religious Thought at the Hebrew Union College–Jewish Institute of Religion in New York. He is the author of thirteen books, including *Renewing the Covenant: A Theology for the Postmodern Jew* (Philadelphia: Jewish Publication Society, 1991). Rabbi Borowitz was the founding editor of *Sh'ma: A Journal of Jewish Responsibility*.

Edward Bristow is Professor of History at Fordham University. He initiated the *Nostra Aetate* Dialogues while Dean of Fordham College at Lincoln Center. He specializes in Modern European History, and his books include *Prostitution and Prejudice: The Jewish Fight Against White Slavery, 1875–1939* (Oxford: Clarenden Press, 1982).

The Rev. Raymond E. Brown was a Sulpician priest and Auburn Distinguished Professor Emeritus of Biblical Studies at Union Theological Seminary in New York. Among his many works *is The Death of the Messiah: From Gethsemane to the Grave* (New York: Anchor Bible Reference Library, Doubleday, 1994).

Rabbi Shaye J. D. Cohen is the Samuel Ungerleider Professor of Judaic Studies at Brown University, where he is also Director of the Program in Judaic Studies. In his scholarly work, Professor Cohen has long been interested in the varieties of Judaism, the relationships of Judaism and Christianity, and the definitions of 'who is a Jew.' His study on *The Beginnings of Jewishness* is scheduled for publication in fall 1998 by the University of California.

Rabbi Michael J. Cook is the Sol and Arlene Bronstein Professor of Judaeo-Christian Studies at Hebrew Union College in Cincinnati, Ohio, possibly the only Jewish seminary ever to require coursework in Christian scriptures as a core element in its rabbinical training. He is currently writing a major work entitled *Removing the Veil: Modern Jews and the New Testament*. Rabbi Cook's other writings include *Mark's Treatment of the Jewish Leaders* (Leiden: Brill, 1978). Among his many memberships is the Executive Board of the Central Conference of American Rabbis.

Michael Fishbane is the Nathan Cummings Professor of Jewish Studies at the University of Chicago and Chair of the Committee on Jewish Studies. He is the author or editor of fifteen books and over 150 articles and reviews in scholarly journals and encyclopedias. Recipient of many scholarly awards, Fishbane has been a Guggenheim Fellow and twice a Fellow of the Institute for Advanced Studies at the Hebrew University of Jerusalem. His most recent book is *The Exegetical Imagination: Jewish Thought and Theology* (Cambridge: Harvard University Press, 1998).

Dr. John Healey is Director of Fordham's Archbishop Hughes Institute on Religion and Culture. He received his Doctorate in Sacred Theology from the Gregorian University and has been active for many years in interreligious dialogue, principally with the Jewish community.

Susannah Heschel holds the Eli Black Chair in Jewish Studies in the Department of Religion, Dartmouth College. She is the author of *Abraham Geiger and the Jewish Jesus* (Chicago: The University of Chicago Press, 1997). Professor Heschel is preparing a study of "When Jesus Was an Aryan: Protestant Theology in Nazi Germany."

Msgr. John P. Meier is Professor of New Testament at Catholic University in Washington, D.C. The first two volumes of his acclaimed *A Marginal Jew: Rethinking the Historical Jesus* (New York:

Anchor Bible Reference Library, Doubleday), have appeared with the subtitles *The Roots of the Problem and the Person* (1991) and *Mentor, Message, Miracles* (1994).

His Eminence John Cardinal O'Connor became Archbishop of New York in 1984 and Cardinal in the following year. He holds a doctorate in Political Science from Georgetown University.

The Rev. Joseph A. O'Hare, S.J., has been President of Fordham University since 1984. He was the editor of the Jesuit weekly, *America*, and holds a doctorate in Philosophy from Fordham University.

The Rev. Byron Shafer is pastor of the Rutgers Presbyterian Church in Manhattan and Associate Professor of Religious Studies at Fordham University. Most recently, he edited and contributed to *The Temples of Ancient Egypt* (Ithaca: Cornell University Press, 1997).

Rabbi Ismar Schorsch is the Chancellor of the Jewish Theological Seminary in New York, where he is also the Rabbi Herman Abramovitz Professor of Jewish History. His books include *Jewish Reactions to German Anti-Semitism, 1870–1914* (New York: Columbia University Press, 1972).

Margaret O'Brien Steinfels is the editor of *Commonweal*, an independent biweekly journal of political, religious, and literary opinion published by Roman Catholic lay people. Ms. Steinfels has written on a variety of subjects including child care, family issues, bioethics, religion and politics, foreign policy, and national affairs. She is the author of *Who's Minding the Children: The History and Politics of Day Care in America* (New York: Simon and Schuster, 1974).

Peter Steinfels was Senior Religion Correspondent for *The New York Times* from 1988 to 1997. He has published widely on topics ranging across religion, politics, and ethics. He is now a Visiting Professor of History at Georgetown University and continues to write a biweekly column for *The Times*. Dr. Steinfels is preparing a book on American Catholicism.

Rabbi Burton L. Visotzky holds the Nathan and Janet Appleman chair in Midrash and Interreligious Studies at the Jewish Theological Seminary. He is author *of The Genesis of Ethics* (New York: Crown Publishing Group, 1996) and *The Road to Redemption*, scheduled for publication in fall 1998. Professor Visotzky has broadcast widely and is a frequent participant in interfaith dialogue.

Robert Louis Wilken is the William R. Kenan, Jr., Professor of the History of Christianity at the University of Virginia. His most recent book is *Remembering the Christian Past* (Grand Rapids: William B. Eerdmans Publishing Company, 1995).